BLACK AUTHORS AND EDUCATION: AN ANNOTATED BIBLIOGRAPHY OF BOOKS

James Edward Newby

Copyright © 1980 by
James Edward Newby
University Press of America, Inc.
P.O. Box 19101, Washington, DC 20036

All rights reserved
Printed in the United States of America
ISBN: 0-8191-0974-6 **(Perfect)**

ISBN: 0-8191-0975-4 **(Case)**

Library of Congress Catalog Card Number: 79-9677

To My Parents

Contents

Preface ix

Acknowledgments xi

Guide to Symbols and Abbreviations xiii

Education Bibliography 1

Notes 83

Selected Bibliography 85

Author Index 87

Title Index 92

About the Author 103

Preface

Several years ago, I was struck by the apparent lack of knowledge of books, particularly in the field of education,[1] published by black authors. Today the concern with and knowledge of black authors, is extremely limited. It is not known whether this is due to difficulty in identifying works by black authors or to their basically different viewpoints which make exclusion desirable. While some sources[2] suggest that the educational orientation of selected black authors differs from that of some influential non-black authors, it is believed that the difficulty in identifying black authors is primarily responsible for such limitations.

One of the chief sources for identifying works by black authors are the published bibliographies. Bibliographies pertaining to black Americans tend to fall into two major categories: (1) bibliographies comprised of works by and about blacks and (2) bibliographies comprised of works by blacks. It should be noted, however, that these two general categories can be further subdivided into subject areas (e.g. Literature, History, Education, etc.), type entry (e.g. books, dissertations, periodicals, etc.), annotated versus non-annotated, and so on.

Bibliographies in the first category emphasize content without attempting to identify the authors. The compiler of such works gives prime consideration to the orientation of the entries. There is a prodigious number of bibliographies in this category.[3]

Bibliographies comprised of works by blacks are far less numerous and the overwhelming majority are in the area of literature and history. None of the bibliographies reviewed focused on books in the field of education by black authors. With the assistance of a University research grant, a research project was undertaken to fill this void.

A major objective of the research was to compile an annotated bibliography of books on education and educational policy by black authors (covering the period from the 1800's to the present) for the purpose of: (1) updating existing knowledge of educational material by black authors; (2) meeting the growing needs of instructional and research programs, particularly in Afro-American studies and fields related to teaching ethnic groups; (3) assisting research scholars, administrators, teachers, students and the public-at-large in identifying literature on education by black authors to possibly facilitate literary integration; and (4) insuring that the role and contributions of Afro-American authors to the intellectual development of this nation will not be "lost, strayed, or stolen."

To accomplish the research objective, a survey sheet along with a cover letter were mailed to individuals, organizations, publishers, and four-year colleges and universities throughout the country to obtain the identity of black authors who had published one or more books on education. The results yielded names of authors whose works encompass a variety of disciplines. Only books in the field of education were included in the bibliography. The works of many authors were omitted because of inadequate verification[4] of the author's ethnic identity.

Undoubtedly many important works by black authors have been overlooked and I would appreciate any information that will enable me to rectify omissions, reference or credit in subsequent editions. Although not purporting to be exhaustive, the bibliography is a viable research tool and a primary source for identifying some black Americans who have contributed to educational theory and practice.

James E. Newby

January 1980
Howard University
Washington, D.C.

Acknowledgments

I am deeply grateful to many people who contributed to this endeavor. I wish, first, to express my appreciation to the Vice President for Academic Affairs of Howard University, Lorraine A. Williams, and the University-Sponsored Faculty Research Program which provided the "seed Money" to implement this project.

A second important group of contributors consist of graduate and undergraduate students and research assistants who participated in the field research and the writing of annotations. In alphabetical order they are: Linda (Khadija) Botts, Roy Butler, Sanza B. Clark (who also provided editorial assistance), Elizabeth S. Gresham, Veronica James, Eugenie Marsh, Deborah Mitchell, Sherrilynn Y. Mitchell, Kim (Clark) Smith, Kennickson P. Thompson. Also, I wish to extend a very special thanks to Audrey E. Thurman for typing drafts of the manuscript and the final copy. Appreciation is also extended to Judith Y. Ellis for her typing assistance during a draft phase of the project.

A third important group of contributors include my colleagues at Howard University whose advice and counsel during the initial phase of the project were helpful and encouraging. In this respect, Earle H. West, a catalyzer of the project, was more than generous in his comments, suggestions, and encouragement. Others include (alphabetically) Sylvia T. Johnson, Faustine C. Jones, Barbara D. Lyles, Michael R. Winston and the Moorland-Spingarn Research Center staff. Also, many colleagues throughout the country contributed by responding to my questionnaire and/or were instrumental in others responding.

The fourth group of contributors consist of many publishers and editors. Of these I am particularly indebted to Jabari Mahiri who directed my attention to useful references, and Carolyn McKee who provided invaluable editorial assistance.

Most of all, I wish to acknowledge the sympathetic support of my wife, Pat, who allowed me to postpone a number of family projects to work on the manuscript. To all the foregoing persons, I acknowledge my gratitude and accept responsibility for any shortcomings in this book.

Guide to Symbols and Abbreviations

*	Ethnic identity was not verified
**	Non-black author
s.l.n.d.	Without indication of date/place of printing

EDUCATION

Abromowitz, Elizabeth A., Ed. *Proceedings from the National Invitational Conference on Racial and Ethnic Data*. Washington, D.C.: Institute for the Study of Educational Policy, 1976.

    This book contains papers presented at the National Conference on Racial and Ethnic Data in Higher Education held in Washington, D.C. in February 1976 and sponsored by the Institute for the Study of Educational Policy. Problems in the collection and interpretation of racial and ethnic data are discussed. Specific measures are proposed to "resolve inconsistencies and conflicts in the data" and to "identify policy questions for which racial and ethnic data in higher education are needed."

    The question and answer session and summaries of the conference workshops are also included.

Anthony, Earl. *The Time of the Furnaces: A Case Study of Black Student Revolt*. New York: The Dial Press, 1971.

    A case study of black student revolt beginning at North Carolina Agricultural Technical College in 1960 through the major college revolts at San Fernando Valley State in 1968. Anthony considers the effects of these revolts on college curricula, racial makeup of faculty and educational opportunities for blacks during the period when revolutionaries continued to be prosecuted.

Arnez, Nancy Levi. *Partners in Urban Education: Teaching the Inner-City Child*. Norristown, New Jersey: Silver Burdett General Learning Corp., 1973.

    Ethnic groups have pushed for their children to be taught solely by members of their own group. This push came from the black quarter in the 1960's. This book discusses undergraduate programs that prepare prospective teachers to teach 'standardized' American.

Arnez believes that teachers in inner-city schools have consistently tried to impose their values and ideas on the children of ethnic groups, without adequately understanding the culture of these children. This handbook offers insights to help the prospective teacher understand the lifestyle of inner-city children. It provides suggestions and classroom techniques for better teaching.

Bacote, Clarence A. <u>The Story of Atlanta University: A Century of Service, 1865-1965</u>. Atlanta, Georgia: Atlanta University, 1969.

This book discusses the various reigns of administrators dating from 1867 up to 1966, including extracurricula activities, student life, and academic and physical developments during the postwar period.

Ballard, Allen B. <u>The Education of Black Folk: The Afro-American Struggle for Knowledge in White America</u>. New York: Harper and Row, 1973.

Ballard traces the white fear of black education to slavery's need for docile and illiterate creatures. He discusses the struggle of men like Woodson, Washington, and DuBois to foster black education. He also analyzes the strengths and weaknesses of black colleges, the bitter experience of blacks on white campuses, racism implicit in curriculum and textbooks, the recent campus rebellions, and the rise of the Third World forces.

An administrator on a predominantly white campus, he criticizes educational leaders for creating an undereducated class in public schools, for patronizing black students by not taking them seriously as human beings or as students, and for setting and implementing low standards.

Banks, James A. <u>Teaching Strategies for Ethnic</u>

Studies. Boston: Allyn and Bacon, Inc., 1975.

This teaching guide provides strategies, concepts, and resources for teaching comparative ethnic studies. Various chapters examine historical perspective and teaching strategies for each major American ethnic group.

_____. Teaching Strategies for the Social Studies: Inquiry, Valuing, and Decision Making. 2d ed. Reading, Mass.: Addison-Wesley Publishing Co., 1977.

The text is primarily concerned with the methods of teaching social sciences at the elementary and junior high school level. Its arrangement reflects the author's theory of social studies: that individuals must learn the skills of decision making which will in turn help them in their personal lives and the society as a whole.

The author's illustrations and arrangement of topics are clear and make a useful guide for beginning teachers.

_____. Teaching the Black Experience: Methods and Materials. Belmont, California: Fearon Pitman Publishers Inc., 1970

An aid to teachers interested in methods, resources, and strategies for teaching the black experience. This book highlights different approaches to effective teaching of race relations and the black experience in North America. The last chapter is an annotated bibliography of resources for teaching the black experience.

_____, and Jean D. Grambs,** eds. Black Self-Concept: Implications for Education and Social Science. New York: McGraw-Hill, 1972.

This book is the outgrowth of a conference held in September 1963 at Tufts University. The purpose of the conference was to explore the various dimensions of black self-concept, to delineate ways in which the school could enhance the self images of black children and thereby increase their academic achievement and emotional growth.

Position papers are by James A. Banks, Jean Dresden Grambs, Cynthia N. Shepard, Donald H. Smith, Alvin F. Poussaint, Carolyn Atkinson, Bradbury Seasholes, Nancy L. Arnez, James A. Goodman and Barbara A. Sizemore. There are differences in opinions, but these differences serve to stimulate actions on the part of educators about the school's role in enhancing the self-perceptions and identities of black youth.

_____, and William W. Joyce,*eds. <u>Teaching Social Studies to Culturally Different Children</u>. Reading, Mass.: Addison-Wesley, 1971.

This book focuses on the teaching skills, knowledge, and attitudes that are helpful in making social studies relevant and exciting for Afro-American, Mexican-American, Puerto Rican-American, American Indian and other children who come from a culture of poverty.

This book explores (1) the basic problems in teaching social studies, (2) classroom strategies for teachers of culturally deprived students, and (3) curriculum and other changes needed to make social studies and other subjects more meaningful for poor and alienated children.

Blackwell, James Edward. <u>Access of Black Students to Graduate and Professional Schools</u>. Atlanta, Georgia: Southern Education Foundation, 1975.

Blackwell examines factors which help and hinder black students applying to graduate and professional schools. Information on scholarships and financial aid programs are also provided.

_____. <u>The Participation of Blacks in Graduate and Professional Schools: An Assessment</u>.

Atlanta, Georgia: The Southern Education Foundation, 1977.

The author analyzes participation rates of blacks in professional schools of law, dentistry and medicine, as well as the distribution of blacks in journalism and allied health in relation to manpower needs and projections thru 1985. Sources of financial aid and admission policies of schools are also given some attention.

Bloom, Benjamin S.,** Allison Davis, and Robert E. Hess.** Compensatory Education for Cultural Deprivation. New York: Holt, Rinehart, and Winston, Inc., 1965.

Following the Civil Rights Act of 1964, the federal government began to sponsor a variety of programs to make up educational losses suffered by the underprivileged in the United States prior to the 1960's. This book describes various federally funded programs designed to overcome shortcomings in learners and to raise their achievement levels, including such programs as head start, tutorial programs, school reorganization, guidance and counseling, and bilingual education.

Bond, Horace Mann. Black American Scholars--A Study of Their Beginnings. Detroit: Balamp Publishing, 1972.

This study is a follow-up to The Search for Talent. Correlating genetic and neo-Darwinian theories, it examines the socioeconomic background of scholars all over the world. Its aim is to show the equalitarian nature of human ability.

_____. Education of the Negro in the American Social Order. Rev. ed. New York: Octagon Books, 1970.

Bond describes the effects of racial segregation on the educational process for blacks, and makes an analogy with the suppression of other groups in world history. He also discusses black's awareness of their mistreatment by American political and social institutions, and their willingness to articulate dissatisfaction.

_____. <u>Negro Education in Alabama: A Study in Cotton and Steel</u>. Washington, D.C.: The Associated Publishers, Inc., 1939.

This study discusses public education for black children of Alabama, with particular emphasis on the social and economic influences on segregated schools. Cotton and steel - two symbols of life in Alabama - were of course, the most important of these influences. <u>Cotton</u> brought the two races to Alabama, determined their distribution in the state, and the relationships between social and economic classes among white persons. <u>Steel</u> is a symbol of change and has dissolved the political combinations in the state, dug up and replanted hundreds of thousands of families, white and black, and concentrated populations and wealth in areas that in 1860 were little more than wilderness.

_____. <u>The Search For Talent</u>. Cambridge: Harvard University Press, 1959.

This short book describes private and public schemes to identify and help talented young people by means of scholarships, loans, federal aid to education, football and basketball scholarships, and standardized tests. It analyzes drawbacks in methods of selection and compares the American and European educational systems.

Bonner, Mary W. <u>Educators' Diagnostic Guidebook and Reference Manual for Problems in Reading - "Helping Johnny to Become a Better Reader"</u>. Emporia, Kansas: Emporia State University Press, 1978.

The title of this book describes its purpose: to help teachers diagnose reading disabilities by using a competency based approach. It should be used with other materials and textbooks. Bonner gives step by step procedures for identifying obstacles preventing progress and establishing an individual program in reading diagnosis and remediation. The manual can also be used for planning workshops in diagnostic reading.

Bonner discusses various tests for recording reading performance, such as the Wechsler Intelligence Scale for Children, Gates-MacGinitie Reading Test, and the Schoolfield's Articulation Test.

Bowles, Frank,** and Frank DeCosta. <u>Between Two Worlds: A Profile of Negro Higher Education</u>. New York: McGraw-Hill, 1971.

This book describes and analyzes the present condition of historically black colleges. Topics discussed include:

1. the origins and development of educational institutions,

2. the limitations of these institutions,

3. the groups of schools which now enroll black students,

4. the broad picture of black higher education,

5. comparisons between historically white colleges and historically black colleges,

6. the future of black colleges.

Boyd, William M. <u>Desegregating America's College: A Nationwide Survey of Black Students</u>. New York: Praeger, 1974.

This survey was conducted during the 1972-1973 academic year on black students at 40 predominantly white institutions of higher learning. Boyd notes relationships between diverse characteristics and backgrounds of the black student and the institution he or she selected to attend. He suggests new perspectives on issues confronting the black student on the desegregated campus.

Brawley, Benjamin Griffith. <u>Dr. Dillard of the Jeanes Fund</u>. New York/Chicago: Fleming H. Revell Co., 1930.

    Dr. James Hardy Dillard has been closely identified with the educational boards in the South. This biography recounts the way he and others attacked the problem of relations between Anglo-Saxons and blacks in the United States. It describes his life-long devotion to two objectives - the educating of the American black and the creating of a better understanding between blacks and whites.

    Dillard's greatest achievement is perhaps the Jeanes teachers fund, organized first in America "to help the little country schools" and to create jobs for black teachers in the South. These teachers, in turn, improved the health conditions and provided instructions in activities of daily living for their black pupils.

_____. <u>History of Morehouse College</u>. Atlanta: Morehouse College Press, 1917. (rpt. College Park, Maryland: McGrath Publishing Co., 1970).

    Morehouse College in Atlanta, Georgia was operated by the American Baptist Home Mission Society of New York for the education of black men. This book highlights the efforts of the Northern Missionary activities to relieve the unorganized conditions in education in the South soon after the Civil War. The author pays tribute to some of the early presidents of the college, and in order to give a total picture, gives some insight into changes in student life since the college began.

Brawley, James Philip. <u>The Clark College Legacy: An Interpretive History of Relevant Education 1869 to 1975</u>. Princeton, New Jersey: Princeton University Press, 1977.

    Clark University, later called Clark College, is remarkable for the commitment it has made to programs relevant to blacks since it was founded in 1869. This book traces this commitment, and the part played by Clark University in the movement of the Freedman's Aid Society of the Methodist Episcopal Church.

    Brawley writes from four decades of personal and intimate involvement with the college, as a teacher, dean of the college, President and President Emeritus, and member of the Board of Trustees.

_____. <u>Two Centuries of Methodist Concern:
    Bondage, Freedom, and Education of Black
    People</u>. 1st ed. New York: Vantage Press, 1974.

    A comprehensive study of the Methodist Church and its role in the social and educational progress of blacks in the United States. The first two parts of the book examine the church's role during slavery and emancipation and its work with the Freedmen's Aid Society up to 1916. The remainder of the book evaluates the church's contribution to the founding of black colleges.

Brazziel, William F. <u>Quality Education for All
    Americans: An Assessment of Gains of Black
    Americans with Proposals for Progressive
    Development in American Schools and Colleges
    for the Next Quarter-Century</u>. Washington, D.C.: Howard University Press, 1974.

    This book describes the strides blacks have made in their drive toward quality education and the interrelationship between education and economic well-being. It examines different kinds of schooling, including networks of metropolitan colleges and cradle schools. Brazziel recommends specific ways in which business, government, schools, and the black community itself, can continue the momentum toward better education for blacks. He strongly urges adoption of more accurate methods of testing minority students and evaluating the work of the schools.

    Brazziel uses the past as a springboard for future hopes of quality education for all blacks in the next quarter century.

Britts, Maurice W. Blacks on White College Campuses. Minneapolis: Challenge Productions, 1975.

   This study concerns itself specifically with the special Metropolitan Teacher Education Program Selection inaugurated for non-white students in the summer of 1968 at Concordia College, St. Paul Minnesota. Unfortunately, the program revealed the lack of skill and foresight with which many predominantly white institutions of higher education have dealt with the needs of the large number of minority students that they massively recruited for their campuses. This study focuses the attempts of the Concordia College administration to carry out the teacher education program.

Brooks, Charlotte Kendrick. They Can Learn English. California: Wadsworth, 1973.

   Brooks believes that if some students coming out of our schools have not learned to speak and write English fluently and correctly, it is not because they cannot learn. Rather, they have not been properly taught. This book provides practical teaching methods which can be helpful not only to English teachers, but to parents and college students as well. The book focuses on literature, reading, language, and composition.

Brown, Charles Allen. The Origin and Development of Secondary Education for Negroes in Metropolitan Area of Birmingham, Alabama. Birmingham, Alabama: Commercial Printing Co., 1959.

   This book investigates the background of secondary education in Birmingham, Alabama, with attention to Afro-American enrollments, courses of study, the qualifications of the teachers, and school funding. The Appendix includes additional information about the purpose of secondary education and various letters relative to the author's research.

Brown, Hugh Victor. E-Qual-ity Education in North Carolina Among Negroes. Raleigh, North

Carolina: Irving-Swain Press, 1964.

Written in the early 1960's, this book explains how equal education in North Carolina and elsewhere has proven costly because it has remained segregated, a fact which, from the beginning of black education, has plagued the consciences of the liberal elements. Brown discusses how liberal elements in North Carolina began the long road toward equality from March 1866 to the 1960's. He emphasizes the programs, as industrial education, blacks are shunted into, and the promotion of inequality.

_____. A History of the Education of Negroes in North Carolina. Raleigh, North Carolina: Irving Swain Press, 1961

This history was the outgrowth of a conference called by North Carolina Newbold at Shaw University to set the stage for many "next steps" in the saga of the black racial equality. It recounts the early history of education for blacks in North Carolina, from the religious instructions of slave, industrial and practical training, and the era of John Chavis, through the influence of Afro-Americans in the State Department and the recent development of industrial and vocational education. It also discusses the influence of philanthropic individuals and organizations, such as the Slater Fund, and Jeanes Fund, Southern Education Board, and General Education Board in the educational process of North Carolina blacks.

Browne, Rose Butler, and James W. English.* Love my Children: An Autobiography. 2nd ed. Elgin, Illinois: David C. Cook Publishing Co., 1974.

Rose Butler Browne, one of seven children in a struggling, impoverished family, grew up in South Boston. Browne goes on to recount her successful quest for a doctorate at Harvard University in the 1930's. An engrossing and candid story of pride and hard work.

Bryant, Spurgeon Quinton. Why I don't Like Bussing.

New York: Vantage, 1973.

    Bryant uses bussing to illustrate one of the primary forms of racial discrimination which has been a dominant factor in American life ever since slaves were imported from Africa. In the early days of education, bussing was for whites only; black students walked. Bussing thus represents an important part of the network of injustices imposed upon blacks, a conflict in which both black and white children are caught. Bryant writes from personal experiences and observations of discrimination, segregation, and injustices.

Bullock, Henry Allen. <u>A History of Negro Education in the South: From 1619 to the Present</u>. Cambridge: Harvard University Press, 1967.

    Bullock traces the history of Afro-American education from 1619 to the present. Seeking to explain the educational and social revolution in American race relations today, Bullock turns to a model of conflict-unintention-accommodation. He selects strategic periods in American history and attempts to identify the "direct intention" and "inherent conflicts" in relations between blacks and whites. He then explores the unintended and contrary interracial practices resulting from this interaction. In each period, blacks and whites learned to accommodate each other on new and higher levels. At each stage of the historical process, developing educational opportunities for blacks in the South made an important contribution.

Burrell, Leon F., and Zacharie J. Clements.** <u>A Survival Kit for Brothers and Sisters Going to Grey Colleges: The Way to Make It Through Higher Education</u>. White Plains, New York: Weilen Press, Inc., 1973.

    In an intimate "big brother" style, Burrell and Clements speak to black students at white colleges. The book offers study skill techniques, verbal skill suggestions, and general academic improvement ideas. A useful book, not only for students, but also for administrators, faculty, and staff who would like to enhance their understanding of minorities and the difficulties they encounter while attending predominantly white institutions.

Caliver, Ambrose. A Background Study of Negro College Students. Washington, D.C.: United States Government Printing Office, 1933.

This book is based on questionnaires sent in the early 1930's to 95 colleges located in 17 states to create an accurate personal profile of black college freshmen and their family histories (number of children, previous college graduates, income and home life).

_____. Education of Negro Teachers. Washington, D.C.: United States Printing Office, 1933. (rpt. Westport, Connecticut: Negro Universities Press, 1970).

A progress report made to the United States Office of Education, on the state of black teacher education in the early 1930's. It notes the need for improvement, as well as progress that had been made in solving some complex problems in educating black teachers. The study surveys elementary, secondary, and college teachers, and studies their degrees, writings, tenure, sex, marital status, salary, and so on.

_____. National Survey of the Higher Education of Negroes, A Summary. Washington, D.C.: United States Government Printing Office, 1943.

This survey describes the deplorable social and economic conditions of higher education for blacks in the 1940's. It urges the passage of federal legislation and makes suggestions for federal government participation in developing high-grade university education for both races. Responsibility for reform is given to the federal government.

_____. A Personnel Study of Negro College Students. New York: Columbia University,

1931. (rpt. Westport, Connecticut: Negro Universities Press, 1970).

This study, undertaken at Fisk University, explores the ways in which education can best serve the needs of the individual and of society. It analyzes the academic progress of black college students, in relation to their social, economic, and intellectual backgrounds, and shows how an understanding of this relationship will help in counselling black students.

The study includes 450 cases of entering Fisk students for the years 1926, 1927 and 1929. Family size, income and community as well as examination scores, are recorded and analyzed.

_____. Secondary Education for Negroes. Washington, D.C.: United States Government Printing Office, 1932.

This work is the result of a three-year study conducted by the Department of Education, on secondary education for blacks: Its organization, curriculum (including some of the more fundamental subjects), extracurriculum, the pupil population, administrative and supervisory problems, personnel, and activities.

_____. Vocational Education and Guidance of Negroes: Report of a Survey Conducted by the Office of Education. Washington, D.C.: United States Government Printing Office, 1938. (rpt. Westport, Connecticut: Negro Universities Press, 1970).

This statistical report surveys the effects of technological growth and social and economic changes in the first quarter of the century on blacks. What is needed, it suggests, is a new equilibrium between education and occupation for blacks. The survey investigates the opportunities and facilities for vocational education and guidance of Afro-Americans in rural and urban communities.

Caldwell, Dista H. The Education of the Negro Child. New York: Carlton Press, 1961.

Originally written as a master's thesis and slightly revised, this book is primarily concerned with how integration or the maintenance of separate schools affects the quality of Afro-American primary and secondary education, and the impact of segregation upon the moral, mental, and social development of the Afro-American.

The author weighs both sides of the argument and concludes that voluntary separate schools is recommended, as a temporary measure, on all educational levels, except perhaps nursery school and college. She feels that an Afro-American can best fulfill himself, his aims, goals, ideals, and needs and gain a better perspective of life if he first attends a voluntary separate school which will teach him self-respect, self-acceptance, self-reliance, a sense of value and a true knowledge of the contribution of the black race to mankind.

Campbell, Thomas Monroe. The Movable School Goes to the Negro Farmer. Tuskegee: Tuskegee Institute Press, 1936.

This semi-autobiographical sketch begins with campbell's early life in Georgia and later efforts to work his way through the school under Booker T. Washington. Then the federal government chose Campbell to operate the first Movable School, a program begun at Tuskegee Institute. The rest of the book outlines the purpose and results of this type of education for rural people, its present scope and influence in this country and abroad, and presents a brief on the future of black rural life.

Cary, Willie Mae. Worse Than Silence: The Black Child's Dilemma. New York: Vantage Press, Inc., 1976.

Worse Than Silence demonstrates how the black child's value system affects his motivation, his discipline and his general involvement at school. Cary presents various teaching strategies which have been shown to be effective over the years, and argues that the black child can be taught once he is induced to settle down to the business of learning in the classroom.

Castañeda, Alfredo,* Richard L. James, and Webster Robbins.* The Educational Needs of Minority Groups. Lincoln, Nebraska: Professional Educators Publications, 1974.

This book consists of three essays on educational and other needs of Mexican-Americans, Black-Americans, and Native American-Indians. The essays were contributed by three scholars, themselves members of these three minority groups who have bridged the gaps between the dominant society and their own societies. This book is useful for those who seek a better understanding of minorities' problems.

Cheek, James E. Higher Education's Responsibility for Advancing Equality of Opportunity and Justice. Washington, D.C.: Institute for the Study of Educational Policy, 1977.

Cheek, President of Howard University, presented this work at the Institute for the Study of Educational Policy's invitational conference, "Advancing Equality of Opportunity: A Matter of Justice," held May 17, 1977. He examines three themes: (1) the close relationship between knowledge and power and between ideas and action, (2) the ways in which universities have evolved historically from "ivory towers" of knowledge to influencing the practical application of that knowledge, and (3) how advancing equality of opportunity and justice for black Americans is within the purview of modern universities. This short book also contains a foreword by Kenneth Tollett.

Clark, Felton Grandison. The Control of State-Supported Teacher-Training Programs for Negroes. New York: Teachers College, Columbia University, 1934.

This book, published in the 1930's, is divided

into two parts: The first analyzes state institutions designed to train black teachers. In the second part, experts make recommendations for the proper functioning of the institutions.

Clark, Kenneth Bancroft, and Lawrence Plotkin.** The Negro Student at Integrated Colleges. New York: The National Scholarship Service and Fund for Negro Students, 1963.

An interesting study of the lives of 509 black students who received financial aid from the National Scholarship Service and Fund for Negro Students. The major findings concern college performance, college experiences, and post-college adjustment.

Clements, Zacharie,** Leon F. Burrell. Profiles: A Collection of Short Biographies. New York: Globe Book Company, Inc., 1975.

This collection of biographies of great Americans is for juvenile readers. Questions are provided at the end of the stories. There is also a section called "Reading First Aid," which can help in answering the reading questions. The book provides explanations and sample exercises as an aid to the student.

Clift, Virgil A., Archibald W. Anderson,** and Gordon H. Hullfish.** eds. Negro Education in America: Its Adequacy, Problems, and Needs. New York: Harper and Row, 1962.

This collection of essays by famous black educators examines the many problems blacks in the United States have in satisfying their right to equal education. Using sociological, anthropological and psychological data, the essays trace the historical development of these problems. Changes and future directions for black education are also discussed.

Clifton, Fred J. Darl. New York: Third Press, 1973.

Using the unusual and interesting format of a series of letters between a fictitious student (Darl) and his English teacher, the author reveals the subtle prejudices and misunderstandings that exist between people of different races and social classes. Gradually, a sense of mutual understanding and respect develops between Darl and his teacher. The author implies that given a line of communication, others can also experience such understanding and respect. There is a lot of subtle humour which adds enjoyment to the reading but which does not take away from the serious message of the book.

Cogdell, Roy Thomas, and K. Sitaram.** <u>Foundations of Intercultural Communication</u>. Columbus, Ohio: Charles Merrill Publishing Co., 1976.

This interesting book about intercultural communication represents a new direction in the art and process of human interaciton. The authors compare and contrast the cultures of Japan, China, India, Africa, and other nations, as well as the minority groups within the United States. They evaluate the cultural contributions of ethnic groups to American society. This book can be used in ethnic and intercultural studies.

Coger, Rick. <u>Developing Effective Instructional Systems</u>. North Quincy, Mass.: Christopher Publishing House., 1975.

Written as a guide to prospective and practicing teachers and as a supplementary text for education courses, this book analyzes and explores various instructional systems. The book is also designed as a supplementary text for courses in education. At the beginning of each chapter, the author presents questions as an aid in identifying the major problem area focused on in that chapter. At the end of chapters 1 through 7, examples from representative subject fields are provided. Work sheets are located after each sample topic to help teachers design instructional systems.

Colson, Edna Meade. *An Analysis of the Specific References to Negroes in Selected Curricula for the Education of Teachers.* New York: Teachers College, 1940.

Starting with the assumption that the United States is a democracy and that a democracy uses its educational system as one way of solving its problems, Colson then argues that schools "should develop those understandings, attitudes, and abilities in children which make for the solution of these problems." For the schools to be able to do this, she maintains, teachers must be made aware of the problems.

After giving a comprehensive description of the "Negro Problem" in America, Colson then examines the degree and quality of the study of blacks in the curricula of teacher education. Chapter 2 discusses provisions for the study of blacks in elementary school courses of study, and chapter 3 discusses blacks in the curricula of teachers' colleges. Numerous tables are included together with an extensive bibliography.

Conley, Houston, Judith Bailey,** Georgia Eugene, June Key,** and Bernard Minnis. *Contingency Planning for a Unitary School System: A Process Guide for School Desegregation.* Nashville, Tennessee: McQuiddy Printing Co., 1977.

This document is designed to help provide contingency plans for a unitary school system in communities where desegregation is being carried out. It examines school personnel, students, community and human relations departments, and other relevant issues in the effort to show that barriers to equal educational opportunities for black children *can* be eliminated.

Cozart, Leland Stanford. *A Venture of Faith: Barber-Scotia College 1867-1967.* Charlotte, North Carolina: Heritage Printers, Inc., 1976.

This book relates the history of Barber-Scotia College during the first century of its service to contemporary issues. This college, which originated after the Civil War, was created for southern Afro-American girls by the Presbyterian Church. The author discusses the different purposes and programs of the college and the calibre of the people who presided over the college. The book is highlighted by photographs.

Crawford, George Williamson. <u>The Talledega Manual of Vocational Guidance</u>. Talladega, Alabama: Talladega College, 1937.

    This book, published in 1937, is addressed to students attending black colleges in the United States. The book is arranged in three sections. The first describes the aims and objectives of vocational guidance, with particular reference to black colleges. The second deals with a selection of careers, which were reasonably open to young black students in the 1930's, with emphasis on the appropriate college course relevant to such careers. The final section contains additional information which may be very helpful in previewing occupational fields.

Cross, Dolores E., Gwendolyn C. Baker, and Lindley J. Stiles,** eds. <u>Teaching in a Multi-Cultural Society</u>. New York: The Free Press, 1977.

    These essays discuss a variety of educational issues, including the student as an immigrant, the intellectual strengths of minority children, and language arts in a multicultural society. This is a helpful book for meeting the demands of teaching in a contemporary multicultural society.

Culp, Daniel Wallace, ed. <u>Twentieth Century Negro Literature: or, a Cyclopedia of Thought on the Vital Topics Relating to the American Negro by One Hundred of America's Greatest Negroes</u>. Naperville, Illinois: J. L. Nichols and Co., 1902.

    When it was published, early in the century, this volume sought to enlighten uninformed whites on the intellectual ability of the Afro-American, to enumerate the contributions of Afro-Americans to American society, and to enlighten Afro-American youth on various ethical, political and sociological questions arising from the race problem. The list of contributors is long and impressive. The book contains many pertinent topics, but pays particular attention to the education of the Afro-American.

Dabney, Lillian Gertrude. *The History of Schools for Negroes in the District of Columbia, 1807-1947.* Washington: Catholic University of American Press, 1949.

    Originally a doctoral dissertation, this book gives a detailed history of black education in the District of Columbia, through the second World War. It covers all levels of schooling from nursery through college and examines the public, private, and parochial schools that existed in the District, as well as various societies concerned with the education of blacks. The author provides numerous tables and detailed illustrations of the subject matter.

Daniel, Walter Green. *The Reading Interests and Needs of Negro College Freshmen Regarding Social Science Materials.* New York: Teachers College, 1942.

    Daniel conducted this study of 1939 and 1940 fall entering college freshmen, while he was at Howard University. It examines their needs, interests, and abilities in the social sciences. Daniel discusses methods and findings, and suggests ways of promoting general and cultural reading.

Dansby, B. Baldwin. *A Brief History of Jackson College: A Typical Story of the Survival of Education Among Negroes in the South.* Jackson, Mississippi: Jackson College, 1953.

    The history of Jackson College, formerly known as Natchez Seminary, begins after the Civil War and proceeds into the 1930's. Various churches such as the Baptist, and the Methodist, saw the dire need for educating blacks in the South and fanatically strove to meet this need. Jackson College was a result of this endeavor. The book highlights several prominent people who associated with the college.

Davidson, Edmonia White. _Family and Personal Development in Adult Basic Education_. Washington, D.C.: National University Extension Association, 1971.

This work was funded by a grant from the Education Office, U.S. Department of Health, Education, and Welfare in a national effort to find ways of eliminating adult illiteracy in the United States. In this volume Dr. Davidson extensively analyzes low income family structure, on the premise that teachers of adult illiterates should enrich their understanding of their students.

_____. _Operation Cope: Family Learning Center Handbook with Mothers who are Heads of Households_. Washington, D.C.: National Council of Negro Women, Inc., 1975.

Operation COPE, established by the National Council of Negro Women, is an experimental project which established two family learning centers in Washington, D.C., from July 1, 1973 to June 30, 1975. The project was designed to serve the needs of low income mothers who were educationally disadvantaged (had had less than eight years of schooling as measured by standardized tests) and were heads of households. This handbook provides information about procedures used in the parent-child, academic, vocational and community programs, in staff development, with the advisory committee and volunteers.

Davis, Allison. _Social Class Influences upon Learning_. Cambridge, Mass.: Harvard University Press, 1948.

In this work, Davis discusses the concept of

socialization of children, and examines certain differences among social classes and cultural groups in the United States. He discusses the cultural definitions of what constitutes the 'good' and the 'bad' of the middle and lower social classes, and examines the impact of these differences on the learning abilities of the children.

Delaney, William H. <u>Learn by Doing: A Projected Educational Philosophy in the Thought of Booker T. Washington</u>. New York: Vantage Press, Inc., 1974.

An informative evaluation of Booker T. Washington's philosophical approach to education: education for the good of life and social significance. Washington believed that for education to be worthwhile it should enable the individual to develop the will and capacity to enrich the whole life of his community by his personal character and attitudes as well as by economic endowment. Delaney also gives a biographical sketch of Washington, to enhance the reader's understanding of Washington's philosophy.

Della-Dora, Delmo,** and James E. House, eds. <u>Education for an Open Society</u>. Washington, D.C.: Association for Supervision and Curriculum Development, 1974.

A discussion of the prospects of an open society in which all people, including ethnic minorities and the aged, are equally and properly represented. The discussion centers around four essential questions: (1) How open is the society presently? (2) Have educational institutions promoted or inhibited the growth of an open society? (3) Can power be exercised in the society to create or maintain openness? (4) What can be suggested to aid the United States in becoming a truly open society?

James A. Banks and Barbara A. Sizemore are among the many contributors to this work.

Derbigny, Irving Antony. <u>General Education in the</u>

Negro College. Stanford: Stanford University Press, 1947. (rpt. New York: Negro University Press, 1969).

This book is the result of field work study conducted by the author during the school year 1942-1943. It describes the general education programs of 20 black colleges during that period and compares their general education programs with other American colleges. On the basis of these comparisons, suggestions are offered about ways in which improvements can be made.

DuBois, William Edward Burghardt, and August Granvill Dill,* eds. The Common School and the Negro American: Report of a Social Study Made by Atlanta University under the Patronage of the Trustees of the John F. Slater Fund. Atlanta: The Atlanta University Press, 1911.

The authors trace the development of the Afro-American common schools, and discuss general conditions in the schools, such as poor teaching facilities, unqualified and incompetent teachers and superintendents, teachers' salaries, poor enrollment of pupils, and poor financial support. On the basis of the findings of the study, the authors project a grim outlook for the schools.

Edwards, Harry. Black Students. New York: The Free Press, 1970.

The author gives an historical account of the black student movement in the United States. He describes the goals, philosophies and directions of the movement in different stages, and the forces and personalities that have helped to shape the movement. He also discusses the relationship which black students have with the black community at large, with American colleges and universities, and with white liberal student coalitions. He advocates the development of black curricula at all levels in the American educational system, as a means of combatting institutionalized racism in American education.

Edwards, Norma S. *A Special Delivery: A Manual For Teachers of Children*. Washington, D.C.: ICAY Publishing Co., 1977.

This well illustrated manual is written for teachers who work with children who have learning problems. The structure of the book follows the pattern of oral communication, beginning with the phoneme - grapheme association and leading eventually to a discussion of written communication. The book includes various classroom techniques and a reading series which can be made to suit individual children.

Edwards, Thomas Bentley. *Attitudes of High School Students as Related to Success in School*. Berkeley, California: University of California Press, 1958.

This work is based on research done in the late 50's on the attitudes of high school students to their school subjects. The study was undertaken with the aim of improving science education by devising ways to "identify and attract students with potential gifts in this area." Attitudes toward the entire range of academic studies are reviewed. Attitudes favorable to science study are compared with attitudes favorable to the study of the humanities, and with attitudes of students showing no inclination towards academic studies, in order to measure the strength of attitudes favorable to science study.

_____. *The Regional Project in Secondary Education: Evaluation of a Program of Cooperative Curriculum Development*. Berkeley: University of California Press, 1956.

The Regional Project in Secondary Education (RPSE) is discussed and evaluated in eight sections. Section 2 desribes a number of programs similar in nature and philosophy, and the need for careful evaluation of these studies. Section 4 describes the method of the RPSE, its history, its finances, and its organization. Sections 5 and 6 tell the story of the RPSE in the eighteen participating schools. Section 7 presents and analyzes additional data, and the final section gives summaries and conclusions.

_____, and Alan B. Wilson.* A Study of Some Social and Psychological Factors Influencing Educational Achievement. Berkeley, California: University of California Press, 1961.

The data in this study are derived from a study conducted in the spring of 1959 of the elementary school children in Berkeley, California. Using this data, the authors were able to determine the differences in social compositions of various elementary schools. The data showed a clear relationship between certain familiar social backgrounds and academic achievement and aspirations. They also suggest ways in which different school milieux might modify this relationship. Chapters two and five analyze the effects of the social factors upon the achievement and educational aspirations of sixth grade boys. The remaining chapters concern an analysis of the joint effects of background, situational factors, and psychological variables.

_____, and Frederick Wirt,* eds. School Desegregation in the North: The Challenge and the Experience. San Francisco: Chandler Publishing Co., 1967.

This book contains case studies of how ten communities, four near New York City and six in California, responded to the challenge of de facto segregation. Using interdisciplinary techniques, the first two chapters put forward a model of political decision-making, and summarize the social and psychological consequences of various ways of grouping children for instructional purposes. The third selection explores the relation between segregation and the aspirations of school boys. The book includes notes on the chapters.

Epps, Edgar G. Black Students in White Schools.

Worthington, Ohio: Charles A. Jones, 1972.

This collection of seven essays by outstanding black educators deals with the rising population of black students attending white colleges and universities in the United States. These students usually differ from the majority of white students in socioeconomic background, career plans, and patterns of behavior. Consequently, the contributors focused on the various problems which black students experience while attending these institutions.

_____. ed. Cultural Pluralism. Berkeley, California: McCutchan Publishing Corporation, 1974.

One of four in a series called "Contemporary Issues" presented by the National Society for the Study of Education, this book examines cultural pluralism and its relation to equality in education. Various authors speak out in favor of cultural pluralism in education, and the goals implied by it.

Particular attention should be paid to the article by Barbara A. Sizemore in which she discusses four important points surrounding the issue of cultural pluralism in America: (1) the meaning of culture, pluralism, and related concepts; (2) the values emanating from the culture; (3) the educational system produced by this value system; and (4) a model for change.

Fisher, Margaret Barrow,* and Jeanne L. Noble. College Education as Personal Development. New Jersey: Prentice-Hall, Inc., 1960.

This interesting book introduces concepts related to the student's personal development during college. The book is divided into three parts. Part one concentrates on understanding oneself, part two focuses on the role of the student, and part three emphasizes choices and values. The book, which contains a comprehensive section of notes on the various chapters, should prove most

most helpful to college students and prospective college students.

Fleming, John E. The Lengthening Shadow of Slavery: A Historical Justification for Affirmative Action for Blacks in Higher Education. Washington, D.C.: Howard University Press, 1976.

The author chronicles key factors in the black experience which impeded or enhanced the struggle for educational equality. The eras of Slavery, the Revolutionary War, Post-Civil War, "Jim Crowism", and the present are examined. Fleming argues persuasively for affirmative action for blacks in higher education.

_____, Gerald R. Gill, and David H. Swinton. The Case for Affirmative Action for Blacks in Higher Education. Washington, D.C.: Institute for the Study of Educational Policy, 1978.

This book is an attempt to answer controversial questions about the legality and viability of affirmative action programs. Part one provides background to affirmative action and discusses past efforts by blacks to obtain equal educational opportunities. Part two briefly examines current affirmative action programs, and part three deals with the current position of black faculty members. Fleming argues that it is the responsibility of the federal government through its various agencies to enforce affirmative action programs "at all levels of society."

Historical documents and executive orders in the appendices should prove useful to researchers.

Foster, Marcus A. Making Schools Work: Strategies for Changing Education. Philadelphia: The Westminster Press, 1971.

A discussion of the various facets of school life, both positive and negative, and ways of making schools live up to their primary function of educating students. Part I considers the reevaluation of institutional goals; Part II looks at the uses of crisis situations to yield positive outcomes; Part III discusses the changes which schools in trouble can expect to undergo; and Part IV looks at the opportunities that arise out of a complex educational system. The book is written from a sociological perspective.

Froe, Otis D., and Otyce B. Froe.* <u>The Easy Way to Better Grades</u>. Rev. ed. New York: Arco Publishing Co., 1976.

    This book is designed to help students develop the skills necessary for succeeding in school. Practical methods of study and learning are discussed and suggested. This book is addressed to both full- and part-time students and is applicable at both high school and college level. Note especially the thirty principles of study and learning that preface the text, as well as section III, which deals with the planning of a study-recreation-work-rest schedule. The text abounds with various illustrations and exercises.

_____, and Maurice A. Lee.** <u>How to Become a Successful Student</u>. New York: Arco Publishing Co., 1959.

    This book is also designed to help students succeed in school. A practical guide to methods of study and learning, it discusses study techniques, effective reading and listening, note-taking, quizzes and examinations, and how to make the fullest use of educational resources and facilities. A useful guide for all students.

Gary, Lawrence E., and Aaron Favors, eds. <u>Restructuring the Educational Process: A Black Perspective</u>. Washington, D.C.: Institute for Urban Affairs and Research, 1975.

    This book is the result of a workshop sponsored jointly by the Institute for Urban Affairs and Research, the Center for the Study of Handicapped

Children and Youth, the School of Education, and
the Institute for Child Development and Family
Life. Three broad areas discussed are: Afro-
American lifestyle and education development,
policy and organizational development in education, and thirdly, curriculum and student development.

Gayles, Ann Richardson, ed. <u>Instructional Planning
in the Secondary School: Selected Readings</u>.
New York: David McKay Co., Inc., 1973.

Designed for prospective high school teachers,
this book explores the importance of instructional
planning, and the relationship between culture and
educational processes. The essays by various
authorities discuss various techniques for instructional planning, processes fundamental to learning
and teaching, and guidelines for achieving a con-
tinuous process in instructional planning, and
other related topics. A text of special interest
to the student-teacher.

_____, and Larney G. Rackley. <u>Proven and
Promising Educational Innovations in Second-
ary Schools</u>. New York: Simon and Schuster,
Inc., 1976.

This work is geared towards "putting educational
theory into practice in a practical method." The
book will prove useful in college and university
classes and seminars which relate to innovations in
secondary education. It is hoped that this book
will motivate school officials to experiment with
different teaching strategies and thus increase
their effectiveness.

Giles, Raymond H., Jr. <u>Black Studies in Public
Schools</u>, New York: Praeger, 1974.

Details the goals, instructional materials and
teacher preparation of twenty-five black studies
programs in large urban school districts in eleven
northern, mid-western, and western states. Shows
how these programs originated, their educational

objectives, how they operate, and how each district measures the effectiveness of its own program.

_____. *The West Indian Experience in British Schools*. London: Heinemann Educational Publishers Ltd., 1977.

This book describes the special educational needs of West Indian pupils as perceived by their teachers, in socially disadvantaged areas. The author has edited tape-recorded interviews with directors and teachers from seventeen schools to provide a fascinating account of the many different assumptions related to the special needs of West Indian pupils, and the teaching strategies designed to address them in multi-racial schools. He offers an analysis of the various issues and concerns that are raised in the interviews, and concludes that, while schools and their neighborhoods are very diverse, there is still an urgent need for broad policy guidelines for minority groups.

Glasgow, Ann Duncan. *Black Leadership in Urban Schools: A Focus on The Nation's Capitol*. Framingham, Mass.: Wellesley Press, 1974.

This book publishes research on the self-perceptions of leadership behavior of black high school principals in Washington, D.C. The study does not report any significant differences between the self-perceptions of leadership between black and white principals. It also shows that black principals see themselves as competent for leadership roles in professionally staffed organizations.

Goodwin, Bennie Eugene. *The Emergence of Black Colleges*. Pittsburgh, Pennsylvania: Goodpatrick Publishers, 1974.

The book gives a brief introduction to the origin of predominantly black institutions of higher education. Included is a list of (all) black colleges, universities and other institutions of higher education, their controllers, location and founding dates.

Gordon, Edmund Wyatt, and Doxey A. Wilkerson.
    <u>Compensatory Education for the Disadvantaged;
    Programs and Practices: Preschool Through
    College</u>. New York: College Examination
    Board, 1966.

The book presents a critical evaluation of compensatory educational programs for disadvantaged children of all races and national origins. In addition, the book focuses on such important issues like the reasons for compensatory education, the recruitment of teachers, preparation and in-service training, curriculum innovation, the role of the parents and the community, and the present inadequate approach to the education of disadvantaged children. On the basis of these variables, the authors discuss the challenges for the future.

Green, Robert Lee. <u>The Urban Challenge: Poverty
    and Race</u>. Chicago, Illinois: Follett
    Publishing Co., 1977.

A survey of the current state of urban problems and recommendations for specific solutions. The author looks into all aspects of the urban challenge including unemployment, housing, health care, education, welfare, law enforcement, finance and power.

_____, ed. <u>Racial Crisis in American Education</u>. Chicago: Follett Publishing Co., 1969.

The various papers in this book examine such issues in urban schools as curriculum, language, community control, teacher training, compensatory education and separatism. The main theme is that minority children can learn and that it is up to the school system to adopt methods which will be successful in teaching all students.

_____, et. al.* <u>The Educational Status of
    Children During the First School Year Following Four Years of Little or No Schooling</u>.
    East Lansing, Michigan: School for Advanced
    Studies Research Services, College of Educa-

tion, Michigan State University, 1966.

This study was undertaken to determine the effects of a short period of formal education on a sample of children from a private school system known as the Prince Edward County Free School Association. These children were previously deprived of formal education, due to the closing of public schools in Prince Edward County, Virginia. It was found that resumed formal schooling brought significant gains in measured intelligence in the sample. There was also a slight increase in measured achievement. Levels of educational and occupational aspiration, it was found, were related to schooling. The students displayed favorable attitudes toward their resumed schooling.

_____, et. al.* The Educational Status of Children in a District Without Public Schools. East Lansing, Michigan: Bureau of Educational Research, College of Education, Michigan State University, 1964.

This cooperative Research Project investigates the backgrounds of the adult and non-adult Afro-American members of the Prince Edward County Community and merges this information with tests and interviews done at a later date. The project addresses the role of formal education in our society. There are two parts to this study. In the first phase, parents and guardians of school-age children are questioned to determine the number of children, their age, their educational level, and the types of school and related experiences they have had in the last four years. The second stage focuses on the effects of the school closing on the educational and social life of the Afro-American community. Chapter 5 deals with conclusions.

_____, et. al.* eds. School Desegregation-Making It Work: A Report to the Rockefeller Foundation. East Lansing, Michigan: College of Urban Development, Michigan State University, 1976.

This book examines various means of successfully carrying out desegregation in the schools. Prominent contributors offer several points of view on a variety of topics, such as the national political stance on busing, the law and desegregation, and the media and how it relates to desegregation. Specific guidelines, as well as leadership and role responsibilities, for school desegregation are discussed.

Greene, Harry Washington. <u>Holders of Doctorates Among American Negroes: An Educational and Social Study of Negroes Who Have Earned Doctoral Degrees in Course, 1876-1943</u>. Boston: Meador Publishing Co., 1946.

A documented survey of Afro-American holders of doctorates during the inquiry period of 1876-1943. It examines the Afro-American doctorates' out-put, achievement, occupational status, and affiliation with professional and learned societies. Factors prohibiting creative scholarship among the black men and women doctors are also touched upon in this informative survey.

Gurin,** Patricia, and Edgar G. Epps. <u>Black Consciousness, Identity, and Achievement: A Study of Students in Historically Black Colleges</u>. New York: John Wiley & Sons, Inc., 1975.

Based on a series of studies conducted on black college campuses from 1964-1970, the book focuses on the consciousness, identity and achievement of the black student on the black campus. The aspects of (1) individual achievement goals, (2) collective achievements as expressed through social action, and (3) the relationship between the previous two and how each are influenced by pre-college family and demographic background, personal motivation, and the students environment are dealt with in great depth in a scholarly manner. Special attention is given to the concept of group as contrasted to individually oriented motivation among black students.

Hankins, Lela Ruth. <u>Biology: A Problem Solving Approach</u>. New York: Carlton Press, 1970.

    Book stresses an inquiry approach for teaching biology to nonscience majors for the purposes of general education. Includes syllabus, laboratory experiments and other student activities.

Harper, Fredrick Douglass. <u>Black Students: White Campus</u>. Washington, D.C.: APGA Press, 1975.

    The book is designed to be a supplementary textbook for counselors and personnel administrators. The author combines both research and case studies to present a comprehensive view of the challenges faced by black students on predominantly white campuses. The references presented at the end of each chapter are extensive and provide good sources for further research in this area.

Harris, Marquis Lafayette. <u>The Voice in the Wilderness</u>. Boston: The Christopher Publishing House, 1941.

    Harris offers a critical evaluation of higher education in this society. He stresses the importance of religious conviction and sensitivity in elementary and secondary teachers, and discusses Afro-American social philosophy.

Harris, Norene,* Nathaniel Jackson, and Carl F. Rydingword.* <u>The Integration of American Schools: Problems, Experiences, Solutions</u>. Boston: Allyn and Bacon, Inc., 1975.

    The authors, writing in an open and lively style, describe and analyze the effects of desegregation and integration in public education. Based upon personal experiences, interviews, newspaper articles, speeches, and insight, this collection of essays focuses on such issues as what happens when black and white children are grouped together and why; busing; and how to establish quality education for blacks in integrated settings. Each section includes a bibliography to facilitate further exploration of the subject matter.

Haskins, James. <u>Diary of a Harlem School Teacher</u>.
    New York: Grove Press, 1969.

    In describing his experience as a Harlem school teacher, Haskins gives brief personality profiles of his students, many of whom live in sub-standard housing and areas infested with drug addicts. The present educational system, Haskins argues, has not been effective in meeting the needs of these students. He suggests that America's educational institutions need to be restructured and reorganized.

_____, ed. <u>Black Manifesto for Education</u>.
    New York: William Morrow, 1973.

    In this book, eminent black educators respond to the white diagnosis of the educational problems of black children. This diagnosis has led to some faulty prescriptions, such as compensatory education. They maintain that the problems encountered by black children in the public schools do not rest with the children, their families or their backgrounds. Instead, they attribute the problem to the school itself, its basic structure and the educational process. Divergent views about the solution of the problems are offered.

Haynes, Carrie Ayers. <u>Good News on Grape Street</u>:
    <u>The Transformation of a Ghetto School</u>. New York: Citation Press, 1975.

    The story of the transformation of a "demoralized" ghetto school in Watts (Grape Street School) into a model learning environment with open classrooms, integrated curriculum, cross-age grouping and staff-in-service training programs. Under the administrative leadership of Carrie Ayers Haynes, principal of the school, this successful transition awarded Grape Street School much attention in such media as <u>Newsweek</u>, the <u>Christian Science Monitor</u>, and <u>National Educational Television</u>.

Haynes, Leonard L., III, ed. <u>An Analysis of the
Arkansas - Georgia Statewide Desegregation
Plans</u>. Washington, D.C.: Institute for Services to Education, 1970.

This book analyzes the state plans for desegregation of higher education, submitted by Arkansas and Georgia and approved by the Department of Health, Education, and Welfare (HEW) as a result of the <u>Adams V. Richardson</u> (1973) case in which ten states were accused of operating dual systems of education. The state plans are not only evaluated in terms of meeting HEW criteria, but questions are also raised as to the relevancy and adequacy of the HEW criteria themselves.

_____, comp. <u>A Critical Examination of the
Adams Case: A Source Book</u>. Washington, D.C.:
Institute for Services to Education, 1978.

This book details the history of the <u>Adams V.
Richardson</u> (1973) case, a class action suit filed by the National Association for the Advancement of Colored People (NAACP) against the Department of Health, Education, and Welfare (HEW) alleging defaults on the part of HEW in its duty to enforce Title VI of the 1964 Civil Rights Act. The defaults concern ten cases in which southern and border states were operating dual systems of education. Haynes' editing and presentation of the legal documents are particularly effective.

Heilman,** Arthur W., and Elizabeth Ann Holmes.
<u>Really Reading</u>. Columbus, Ohio: Charles E.
Merrill Publishers, 1976.

This book draws together a variety of word roots, phrase reading, vocabulary, and conceptual knowledge useful to students. The companion workbook is designed for a developmental reading skills program, effective in enhancing independent reading skills as well as supplementing standard curriculum through individualized instruction.

_____. <u>Smuggling Language into the Teaching</u>

37

of Reading. Columbus, Ohio: Charles E. Merrill Publishing Company, 1972.

Why are so many children not learning to read? This text demonstrates different skills and methods for making reading meaningful to children. One technique is to "smuggle" language into reading and make it as attractive to the child as possible. Each chapter contains actual exercises as examples of how child participation in language can be an incentive to reading.

Henderson, George. Introduction to American Education: A Human Relations Approach. Norman, Oklahoma: University of Oklahoma Press, 1978.

This is an up-to-date review of the major sociocultural forces affecting American education. It is interdisciplinary in its approach and draws from sociology, psychology and anthropology in addition to studies in the field of education. The author emphasized current problems in planning curricula for today's students, with special emphasis being placed on human rights issues: racism, sexism, cultural pluralism, and student rights. Separate chapters are dedicated to drug and alcohol abuse. This book provides data, techniques, and strategies for the improvement of school conditions.

_____, comp. America's Other Children: Public Schools Outside Suburbia. 1st ed. Norman, Oklahoma: University of Oklahoma Press, 1971.

Focusing on rural schools and small communities, the author attempts to bridge the gap between rural and urban schools. "Problems of Disadvantaged Youth, Urban and Rural," "The Schools of Appalachia," "What Migrant Farm Children Learn," "The Desegregation of Southern Schools: A Psychiatric Study" are among the fifty-one articles. The book is divided into six parts with an introduction to each part.

_____, ed. Education for Peace: Focus on Mankind. Washington, D.C.: Association for Supervision and Curriculum Development, 1973.

Presupposing a need for greater commitment to peace, this book includes literary references and statistical data that can present a framework for the improved effectiveness of educators for peace. The book discusses the implications for education making a comprehensive study of relationships between man and his total environment, and other issues. Appendixes A,B,C,D, comprise: Data on the Human Crisis; Teacher's Guide; Selected Bibliography on International Education; Additional Resources and Consortium on Peace Research; Education and Development.

_____, and Robert F. Bibens.** Teachers Should Care: Social Perspectives of Teaching. New York: Harper and Row, 1970.

This book contains information and teaching techniques useful to both students and teachers. It discusses the importance of grade transfers; the ways school records affect reputations; parent-teacher conferences; discipline; and goals for better human relations.

Hendrick,** Irving G., and Reginald Lanier Jones, eds. Student Dissent in the Schools. Boston: Houghton Mifflin, 1972.

This book examines the relationship between activist-students and personnel in public secondary schools. The final chapter, "Directions for the Future," should prove most helpful to educators.

Hesburgh,** Theodore Martin, Paul A. Miller,* and Clifton R. Wharton, Jr. Patterns for Lifelong Learning. 1st ed. San Francisco: Jossey-Bass Publishers, 1973.

This volume grew out of a project conducted at the University of Notre Dame by several task forces on continuing education and the authors. The major sections are entitled: Continuing Education and the

Future, Universities and the Learning Society, and the Lifelong University. An attempt to present broad effective educational ideas and systems, this book is of great value to educators and the general public.

Holley, Joseph Winthrop. <u>Education and the Segregation Issue: A Program of Education for the Economic and Social Regeneration of the Southern Negro</u>. New York: William-Frederick Press, 1955.

Holley discusses the historical and philosophical implications of state-supported education for blacks in a segregated milieu, and argues that economic and social regeneration of blacks must begin in the earliest years of education.

Holmes, Dwight Oliver Wendell. <u>The Evolution of the Negro College</u>. New York: Arno Press, 1969.

Using primary sources, Holmes examines the conditions under which the black college was founded and studies the agencies primarily responsible for their development. The manuscript was Holmes' doctoral dissertation completed at Teacher's College, Columbia University.

Hudson, Herman C., ed. <u>How to Make it in College</u>. Bloomington, Indiana: Indiana University Press, 1976.

A useful guide for college students, this book provides basic facts about dormitories, dating, drugs, I.Q. tests, program planning, effective study procedures, financial aid, counseling and tutorial services. Included also are student exercises on budget making, term paper preparation, and techniques for job interviews. Real life problems are illustrated by biographical sketches of students.

Hunter, William Andrew, ed. <u>Multicultural Education Through Competency-Based Teacher Education</u>.

Washington, D.C.: American Association of Colleges for Teacher Education, 1974.

This book provides a social and historical view of education with an emphasis on multicultural education; it examines multicultural education from a black perspective and looks at some native American views on this topic. Finally the book provides a cross-cultural approach to multicultural education and examines what our next steps in this area will be.

Hurst, Charles G., Jr. <u>Passport to Freedom, Education, Humanism and Malcolm X</u>. Hamden, Connecticut: Linnet Books, 1972.

To counteract the effects of racism on black youth in America, the educational structure has to be revitalized to meet the needs of black American youth. Malcolm X College, inspired by the humanistic message of Malcolm X on education for blacks, is presented as an example of how creative efforts on the part of competent persons can help to produce an environment suitable for developing human potential.

Jackson, John Henry. <u>History of Education from the Greeks to the Present Time</u>. Denver: Western Newspaper Union, 1903.

The author covers the development of education over a period of 2,000 years beginning with the Greeks. He also includes biographical data on such noted black educators as Booker T. Washington, Richard Wright, Peter Clark and Lucy Moten.

Johnson, Charles Spurgeon. <u>Education and the Cultural Crisis</u>. New York: MacMillan Co., 1951.

Johnson focuses upon cultural aspects of education found in schools. He argues that our schools tend to support the dominant cultural pattern of education while ignoring other cultural patterns. He recommends ways of counterbalancing this bias.

_____. *The Negro College Graduate*. Chapel
   Hill: University of North Carolina Press,
   1938.

   This book publishes the results of a study
conducted by the General Education Board on the
objective records of college and professionally
trained blacks in the United States from 1826-1936.
Its statistical data covers the number, distribution, and occupational adjustment of the black
graduates of colleges, professional, and vocational
schools.

   Johnson analyzes in detail particular social
factors which influence the number and status of
black graduates. He also examines existing educational methods and aims in higher education, and
suggests educational modifications. He lists
producers and distributors of multimedia materials
on the Afro-American and the peoples of Africa.

Johnson, Harry Alleyn. *Multimedia Materials for
   Afro-American Studies: A Curriculum Orienta-
   tion and Annotated Bibliography of Resources*.
   New York: R.R. Bowker Co., 1971.

   This volume discusses ways of relating new
technological and educational media to the ghetto
youth and of integrating black studies, especially
Afro-American history, in the curriculum. It also
explores the sociological and psychological needs
of ghetto youth.

Johnson, Kenneth R. *Teaching the Culturally Disadvantaged: A Rational Approach*. Palo Alto,
   California: Science Research Associates, 1970.

   Johnson's primary concern is to provide teachers of culturally disadvantaged children with
some meaningful guides in this area. His suggestions
are stimulating and useful.

Johnson, Roosevelt, ed. *Black Agenda for Career
   Education*. Columbus, Ohio: ECCA Publications, 1974.

In this anthology scholars and thinkers, including William F. Brazziel, Melvin Sikes and Joseph Discon, duscuss pertinent issues surrounding career education. References are made to evaluation and career education, the development of institutional goals in a public school system, and adaptation of the career education concept to correctional settings.

_____, ed. <u>Black Scholars on Higher Education in the 70's</u>. Columbus, Ohio: ECCA Publishers, Inc., 1974.

This collection of articles by the author and other prominent blacks in higher education addresses diverse issues, ranging from compensatory programs for blacks to higher education for black inmates. This book is of special interest to policy makers in the area of student development, research, administration, and personnel development.

Johnson, Simon Otis. <u>Good Morning Mrs. "B"</u>. Dubuque, Iowa: Kendall and Hunt, 1973.

Based on his own experience as a principal in an integrated school system, Johnson has given us what is really a novel about a new teacher's first year working with students from different cultural backgrounds. Somewhat inept, Mrs. "B" allows one student to disrupt the entire class, and follows his edicts without even being aware that she is doing so. Unfortunately it is very difficult for Mrs. "B" to see the need to change her teaching style. The book illustrates that although need for a change in teaching styles may be obvious to many others, it does not occur unless the teacher herself sees a need for it.

_____. <u>Multicultural Elementary Classrooms</u>. Dubuque, Iowa: Kendall and Hunt, 1972.

This book serves as a guide for both teachers and prospective teachers in the following respects: (1) to help teachers in developing curricula for

children in a multicultural setting, (2) to make
teachers aware of barriers to effective teaching
and learning brought on by their lack of understanding of cultural differences among children
and between themselves and children and, (3) to
set forth the paradigms of value in resolving
classroom problems. The book depicts five classroom situations familiar to most teachers, and
suggests solutions to these situations. The book
also includes a rating scale of ten teaching
characteristics with a general explanation of
each. This is intended to motivate the teacher
to seek additional help in the areas he or she
identifies as being weak.

Johnson, Sylvia T. The "Measurement Mystique":
  Issues in Selection for Professional Schools
  and Employment. Washington, D.C.: Institute
  for the Study of Educational Policy, 1979.

Do the selection methods used by schools
accurately predict performance in the first and
second years of school? Can these methods determine the calibre of the applicant upon completion
of school? According to Johnson, tests are necessary, but educational and vocational decisions cannot depend entirely on them, since the tests do
not accurately assess the aptitude of all students,
especially minority students. Inspired by the
Bakke (1978) case, Johnson carefully discusses the
admissions procedures of various medical schools:
GPA, MCAT scores, faculty recommendations, socioeconomic and demographic ratings, and other factors
such as personality and direction of interest.
She examines the origins and identification of test
bias in the United States, and recommends modifications in selection procedures for professional
schools.

Jones, Edward Allen. A Candle in the Dark: A
  History of Morehouse College. Valley Forge,
  Pennsylvania: The Judson Press, 1967.

The story of Morehouse College is the story
of higher education for many Afro-Americans in the
deep South, and of the social, political, and eco-

nomic difficulties they faced and continue to face. This history can boast of its success in creating men of worth and psychological freedom who have contributed in a significant manner to their environment.

Included are photographs of presidents of Morehouse College and of some of the buildings and social events relating to the college. The book concludes with a list of some one hundred and seventeen Morehouse graduates who have earned doctorates.

Jones, Gilbert Haven. Education in Theory and Practice. Boston: R. G. Badger, 1919.

This book discusses various theoretical and practical aspects of traditional education systems, including the concept of education, the nature and objectives of education, and methodology.

Jones, Leon. From Brown to Boston: Desegregation in Education, 1954-1974. 2 vols. Metuchen, New Jersey: The Scarecrow Press, Inc., 1979.

This two volume work comprises literature on desegregation in Education covering the period from the historic Brown decision in 1954 to the Milliken vs. Bradley ruling in 1974 and the Boston busing crisis of the same year. In addition to a foreword by Roy Wilkins, volume I contains an introduction which represents the author's "views on the issues and the problems of school desegreation" during the twenty year period under consideration. The bulk of the volume consists of a bibliography of summarized articles and books pertaining to school desegregation. Volume II contains summaries of legal cases reported in Race Relations Law Reporter, and Race Relations Law Survey. Appendixes, containing Brown, Milliken, and indexes are also included. Together the two volumes include "over 5000 summary statements" covering more than 2000 pages.

Jones, Reginald Lanier. New Directions in Special Education. Boston: Allyn and Bacon, Inc., 1970.

A collection of essays on trends and developments in special education for teachers in special education, administrators, counselors, and as a textbook in advanced courses in education and psychology of exceptional children. This four-part book presents teaching methods, and readings on curriculum and teaching, technology, and federal programs concerned with the exceptional child.

_____, ed. Problems and Issues in Education of Exceptional Children. Boston: Houghton Mifflin, 1971.

The essays focus on controversial issues and problems pertaining to the education of exceptional children. The volume also covers the field of handicapped children.

_____, and Donald L. MacMillan,** eds. Special Education in Transition. Boston: Allyn and Bacon, Inc., 1974.

This collection of articles explores new perspectives in the area of special education. Various authorities focus on a wide range of issues, such as alternative curriculums, the use and abuse of educational categories, "tracking", and the integration of exceptional children into regular classes.

Very informative; a reading must for educators and students in special education.

Kimmons, Willie James. Black Administrators in Public Community Colleges: Self-Perceived Role and Status. New York: Carlton Press, Inc., 1977.

How do black educators see themselves and their positions of authority in local colleges? Kimmons examines the personal and professional backgrounds

of black administrators, and brings out some
interesting findings. The black administrators
generally felt their salaries were below average
when compared to administrators in predominantly
white institutions. The social perspective this
study presents is good food for thought, and indeed,
all aspects touched upon in these pages are worthy
of consideration.

Knox, Ellis O. *Democracy and the District of Columbia Public Schools: A Study of Recently Integrated Public Schools*. Washington, D.C.: Judd & Detweiler, 1957.

    A 1957 study of the integration of District
of Columbia Public Schools. Knox describes the
inequities of segregated schools, the D.C. public
school testing program, health hazards, and the
effects of accelerated migration on D.C. public
schools.

LeMelle, Tilden J., and Wilbert J. LeMelle. *The Black College: Strategy for Achieving Relevancy*. New York: Praeger, 1969.

    Particular areas of interest in this study
are the following: The development of these institutions; an ideology for black educational development; a design for institutional administration,
faculty and student re-evaluation and renewal; the
problem of support for black colleges; the future
of black colleges and their effects on the black
community and black/white relations; as well as
the influence of education in black colleges on
a pluralistic democracy.

Lewis, James, Jr. *Administering the Individualized Instruction Program*. West Nyack, New York: Parker Publishing Co., Inc., 1971.

    Lewis focuses on individualized instruction
as a way of making the education process more
effective and relevant to the concerns of special
students. He takes into account differences in
levels of ability, rates of learning, and learning

goals. Understanding these differences is important to reforming liberal education.

_____. *Appraising Teacher Performance*. West Nyack, New York: Parker Publishing Co., 1973.

In this book, Lewis examines the necessity for teacher appraisals, alternative approaches (as well as his own), and ways of carrying out his learning-center approach and appraisal. Lewis devotes several chapters to personal and professional skills and objectives, and the use of motivation and perception for improving teacher performance.

_____. *The Tragedies in American Education*. New York: Exposition Press, 1971.

According to Lewis, the tradegy in American education is the public educational system which perpetuates an outdated curriculum and an antique teacher training system. Other ills, says Lewis, are lack of federal and state financial support and a dearth of effective parent involvement in the schools. The greatest tragedy, Lewis believes, is the effect all of this has on the child.

Lightfoot, Sara Lawrence. *Worlds Apart*. New York: Basic Books, Inc., 1978.

This volume explores the complex relationship between American families and schools, and the conflicts and tensions, as well as the harmonies, of this relationship. Lightfoot brings in diverse viewpoints, including those of institutions, social structures, teachers, and parents. She places the present state of school-family relationship in historical perspective, and asks us to see this relationship in terms of its roots in the sociopolitical and cultural history of America. Lightfoot offers suggestions for the direction our educational institutions might take in the future.

Logan, Rayford Whittingham. <u>Howard University</u>:
 <u>The First Hundred Years 1867-1967</u>. New York:
 New York University Press, 1969.

   Logan discusses the growth and development
of this institution during the administration of
Mordecai W. Johnson (1926-1960). It was during
this time that Howard University was awarded full
accreditation. Logan also gives us brief biographies of many faculty and graduates who attained
prominance in local, national, and international
affairs, including Charles H. Houston, William
H. Hastie, James Nabrit, and Ralph J. Bunch. Of
particular interest is Logan's discussion of
Howard University's involvement in International
Activities and Civil Rights Movements (1867-1967).

Maupin, Madeline Taylor. <u>Peer Group Counseling</u>
 <u>Policies and Human-Relations Workshops</u>
 <u>Procedures</u>. Louisville, Kentucky: Printing
 Needs - Lincoln Foundations, Inc., 1975.

   This book surveys procedures for conducting
Peer Group Counseling and Student Human Relations
Workshops. It includes letters of recommendations
and various forms used to implement successful
guidance programs. Student comments before and
after workshop experiences, newspaper stories, and
pictures are also included. The material in this
book is the result of actual guidance experiences
tried and evaluated in a predominantly black/innercity secondary school.

Mays, Benjamin Elijah. <u>Born to Rebel</u>. New York,
 New York: Charles Scribner's Sons, 1971.

   This autobiography is dedicated to young
people today who cannot have any idea of early
black-white relations in the south. It tells of
one man's determination to preserve his pride and
dignity in a hostile society, and of his arduous
attempt to become educated against almost overwhelming odds. Pictures of the author at different
periods in his life, and a helpful appendix are
also included.

Mays, Robert E., compiler. Opening the Public
    School Curriculum. Dubuque, Iowa: Kendall/
    Hunt, 1976.

   This book, designed for teachers of graduate
and undergraduate courses, is divided into three
parts: "Openness in the Classroom," "The Nature
of Openness," and "Now and Beyond." Many noteworthy
advocates of open education have contributed
articles. In the first selection, Ronald Baret
argues for a philosophical commitment to the assumptions of open education. Other articles discuss
operating principles of the open classroom and the
complex nature of educational change. The book
also reviews selected literature on open education.

_____. Supervising Student Teachers: A
    Practical Approach. Kendall/Hunt Publishing
    Co., 1978.

   This handbook gives a general overview of
teacher education at Indiana State University in
Evansville. It outlines the role of each member
of a supervisory team, and discusses the limitations and responsibilities imposed by legal requirements and policy. The appendix presents evaluation and other special forms.

McAllister, Jane Ellen. The Training of Negro
    Teachers in Louisiana. New York: Columbia
    University, 1929.

   This 95 page text is based on a 1929 survey
of black teacher training agencies in the state
of Louisiana, including Southern University, and
Leland and Straights Colleges. McAllister discusses
factors affecting the program, such as the supply
and demand of black teachers. She evaluates the
agencies, and recommends remedial measures.

McKinney, Richard Ishmael. Religion in Higher
    Education Among Negroes. New Haven: Yale
    University Press, 1945.

   McKinney examines the history of the relationship between religion and higher education for blacks in the United States; the attitudes of eighteen presidents of black colleges toward religion in higher education during 1940-41 school year; the extent of religion in curricula; and student attitudes towards religion. The appendix includes all the colleges which contributed in some form to the study. An extensive bibliography is provided for those interested in further research in this area.

McKinney, Theophilus Elisha, ed. <u>Higher Education Among Negroes</u>. Charlotte, North Carolina: Johnson C. Smith University, 1932.

A collection of addresses delivered at the 25th anniversary of the presidency of Dr. Henry Lawrence McCrorey of Johnson C. Smith University, by such notables as Carter G. Woodson and Mary McLeod Bethune. The speakers discuss Afro-American education in the twenty-five years prior to 1932, the situation in 1932, and what education will probably be like in the next twenty-five years. Contemporary scholars of Afro-American higher education will be interested in comparing their projections, made sixty years ago, with what has actually taken place in the decades since the thirties.

Mercer, Walter Alexander. <u>Humanizing the Desegregated School: Guide for Teachers and Teacher Training</u>. New York: Vantage Press, 1973.

This book is particularly pertinent to students in elementary and secondary teacher training institutions. It looks at the difficulties of desegregating Southern schools, and the effects of desegregation on teachers, training programs, and relationships between the teacher and the principal.

_____. <u>Teaching in the Desegregated School: Guide to Intergroup Relations</u>. New York: Vantage Press, 1971.

Many books have been written on education of

black and white Americans. This book looks at <u>teacher</u> education in desegregated schools. Mercer tries to make teachers aware of their importance in moulding young minds, and of the harmful effect of holding prejudices, whether conscious or not, against the ethnic cultures of their students.

Miller, LaMar P., ed. <u>The Testing of Black Students</u>: <u>A Symposium</u>. Englewood Cliffs, New Jersey: Prentice-Hall, 1974.

This symposium began with the assumption that the most controversial and complex issue affecting the education of minorities in America today is the role of educational and psychological testing. The ten contributors review specific issues connected with testing, such as "The Latent Functions of Intelligence Testing in the Public Schools" (by Jane Mercer), and the heredity versus environment issue (by Lawrence Plotkin). Questions raised include: how tests predict and measure school achievement, the situational effects of testing, and to what extent tests should be diagnostic or evaluative.

_____, and Edmund W. Gordon, eds. <u>Equality</u> <u>of Educational Opportunity</u>: <u>A Handbook for</u> <u>Research</u>. New York: AMS Press, Inc., 1974.

This compilation is designed to inspire more research on equality of educational opportunity. Material is presented in two historical frameworks: first, the history of American education, through which equality can be achieved; and, second, the development of educational research in the United States. The editors argue that complex problems remain to be solved.

Moore, William, Jr. <u>Against the Odds</u>. 1st ed. San Francisco: Jossey-Bass, Inc., 1970.

The subject of this book is the so-called "high risk" or marginal student, and the difficulties he faces in a community college. Both the "high risk" student and the two-year college, which often has the reputation of being a "remedial learning situation," are struggling with what might be called a crisis of identity. Little research has been done on the characteristics of the marginal students. But we know that faculty members at two-year colleges are often torn between adjusting the curriculum to accommodate the "high risk" students, and upholding the academic standards of the institution, which sometimes means expelling the ill-equipped students.

_____. *Blind Man on a Freeway*. San Francisco: Jossey-Bass, 1971.

Moore examines the crucial problems and issues facing the two-year college administrator and advocates more effective training for the professional educational administrator. He discusses the effect of emerging groups, such as militants, minorities, and the educationally disadvantaged students on the campus community. Collective bargaining problems are also touched upon.

_____. *Community College Response to the High-Risk Student: A Critical Reappraisal*. Washington, D.C.: American Association of Community and Junior Colleges, 1976.

Community colleges claim success in remediating high-risk students, so that these students can make normal academic progress. Appraising this claim, Moore points up the lack of hard evidence supporting it, and contends that the problem of the poor academic achiever remains even beyond the community college. Moore suggests that community colleges reevaluate their policies on the achievement problem and take a new and closer look at their general response to high-risk students.

_____, and Lonnie H. Wagstaff. *Black Educators in White Colleges*. 1st ed. San Francisco: Jossey-Bass, 1974.

The book is based on a survey of black faculty and administrators in white colleges and universities that included responses from both black and white faculty administrators and university heads.

The book is a provocative and enlightening survey of the problems and prospects of the black educator and administrators on the white campus.

Moseley, Clifton L. *The Torch Glows*. New York: Carlton Press, 1966.

This study, undertaken in DeSoto County, Mississippi, covers a twenty-year period. The book begins with historical sketches of DeSoto County. Moseley discusses the educational background of blacks in DeSoto County, and one of the County's important institutions, the Baptist Industrial School. Moseley also discusses educational principles and policies in a segregated school system, and examines such issues as faculty, students, testing and the classroom. The book is illustrated with pictures of the school.

Muhammad, Farid I. *Islamic Social and Educational Issues*. Chicago: World Community of Islam in the West, 1977.

Muhammad argues that Al-Islam, in general, and Islamic education, in particular, can improve the state of the Bilalian (black) community of North America. Each chapter begins with a brief history followed by an analysis of why secular and non-Islam societies have failed to improve the situation and finally why Al-Islam is the best alternative. Underlying Muhammad's arguments is the assumption that no distinction should be made between secular and religious education. "The educational system, as viewed from an Islamic social context," says Muhammed, "has a primary responsibility in facilitating the careful cultivation and natural growth of (the) moral and spiritual quality in man."

Napper, George. *Blacker Than Thou: The Struggle for Campus Unity*. Grand Rapids: William B. Eerdmans, 1973.

This book examines the political world of the black college student and analyzes his situations in predominantly white institutions of higher learning, and attempts to present a new perspective on student unrest during the black student movement.

Topics covered are the politics of becoming black, how to get it together at Berkeley, and the relationship between black men and women. Napper speaks directly from the author's experiences as a black administrator at the University of California at Berkeley.

Newton, James E. A Curriculum Evaluation of Black Studies in Relation to Student Knowledge of Afro-American History and Culture. San Francisco: R and E Research Associates, 1976.

Newton evaluates the effectiveness of black studies in teaching Afro-American history and culture. Newton uses ninety-two male and female undergraduate students, and two samples consisting of the black studies curriculum group and the traditional curriculum group. He provides an inventory of Afro-American knowledge, with questions to test the reader's familiarity with Afro-American history and culture.

Neyland, Leedell Wallace, and John W. Riley.* The History of Florida Agricultural and Mechanical University. Gainesville: University of Florida Press, 1963.

Neyland and Riley trace the history of A & M University from its founding seventy-five years ago to what they describe as its present day success as a career school. The text includes illustrations and appendixes, with lists of former graduates who later obtained terminal degrees, as well as those who became successful in the sports arena such as All-American football.

Noble, Jeanne L. The Negro Woman's College Education. New York: Teacher's College, Columbia University, 1956.

This book is the result of a 1956 study of black women with four or more years of college education. The history of black education, demographic data, the motivations for this education as well as the types of education sought and received by black women are discussed. Noble's discussion of educational priorities and the benefits of education for women is clearly a product of the fifties. But, although dated, the text explores areas which are still relevant to black women (and men) today.

Ornstein,* Allan C., Daniel U. Levine,** and Doxey A. Wilkerson. Reforming Metropolitan Schools. Pacific Palisades, California: Goodyear Publishing Co., 1975.

The central question of this book is whether public schools are providing adequate education for economically deprived children who attend schools in predominantly low income urban area. The major issues, each treated in a separate chapter, are compensatory education, educational accountability, decentralization and community control, and desegregation.

Payne, Charles Ray. Multi-Cul: Programs for the Preparation of Teachers for Multi-Cultured Secondary Schools. Muncie, Indiana: Ball State University, 1976.

In this brief discussion of the teacher education program at Ball State University (Muncie, Indiana), Payne demonstrates the success of the program in training teachers to be more effective in multicultural classrooms.

_____, and Dennis Redbury,** eds. Multicultural Education Clinic Papers. Muncie, Indiana: Ball State University Teachers College Publication, 1976.

This book examines various aspects of multicultural education, such as program and curriculum. It studies blacks and other minorities in American schools, and provides an interesting summary of the 1975 conference on multicultural education.

Perry, Thelma Davis. History of the American Teachers Association. Washington, D.C.: National Education Association, 1975.

Perry describes the subtle methods used by a group of black teachers to undermine the racist educational system. The book deals with the successes and failures of the group as a whole, and includes speeches, papers, quotations of the American Teachers Association, and state bulletins and periodicals. The appendix has descriptions of outstanding past presidents.

Phillips, Carol, ed. Collective Monologues I: Toward A Black Perspective in Education. California: Stage 7/Pacific Oaks College, 1976.

This collection of articles was published by Stage 7, a coalition of black educators in California. Biographical information on the contributors is included.

Picott, John Rupert. History of the Virginia Teachers Association. Washington, D.C.: National Educational Association, 1975.

Virginia Teachers Association rose to national recognition as one of the most effective forces for educational reform in Virginia. This history traces the Association from its inception as a source of Afro-American school leaders, to its coalition with the more broadly based Virginia Education Association. The policies of the organization are included, together with profiles of a few of its outstanding leaders and personalities. There are numerous photographs.

_____. A Quarter Century of the Black Experience in Elementary and Secondary Education, 1950-1975. Washington, D.C.: Picott, 1976.

A short history of black education at the elementary and secondary levels. This book discusses the values of these school systems in the context of American educational goals which are often middle class and oblivious to the needs of blacks. Key issues discussed are desegregation, busing, government and education, black studies, black English, and, of course, testing. The text includes photographs of some prominent black individuals and offers projections for the future of black education up to the year two thousand.

Pruitt, Anne S. New Students and Coordinated Counseling. Atlanta, Georgia: Institute for Higher Educational Opportunity, Southern Regional Education Board, 1973.

In this report on coordinated counseling in traditionally black colleges, Pruitt conducts a case study of a new student on a predominantly white campus. The report puts forward a case of a coordinated counseling program, and discusses traditionally black colleges in terms of staffing patterns, relationships between coordinated counseling programs and other units of the institution. The report aims to increase the effectiveness of black colleges in serving the needs of their students. Includes diagrams.

Ragan,* William Burke, and George Henderson. Foundations of American Education. New York: Harper & Row, 1970.

Designed primarily for the first year education student this text focuses on the factors and forces in society which affect American education. Attention is also directed to the problem of the poor, innovative programs, new perspectives in human growth and learning, and lastly, to projections of changes likely to occur in the future. As background material, this test is of general interest to social science students.

Rembert, Emma White. Alternative Strategies: Reading in the Elementary School. Dubuque, Iowa: Kendall/Hunt Pub. Co., 1976.

This spiral bound booklet of 68 pages presents a coordinated set of nine modules designed as a course guide for teachers. It contains competencies to be developed, trainee tasks, enabling activities, and suggested instructional resources for each module. It also contains references for teacher study, selected list of teaching material for pupils, and a list of tests useful for developing diagnostic shells.

Richmond, Mossie J., Jr. Issues in Year-Round Education. North Quincy, Mass.: The Christopher Publishing House, 1977.

This book attempts to resolve the wide range of difficulties relating to year-round education. Richmond identifies extended school year or year-round school programs in the United States, and discusses the rationale for the extended school year, problems in administration, sources of additional revenue, and community acceptance of these programs.

Rodgers, Frederick A. Curriculum and Instruction in the Elementary School. New York: MacMillan, 1975.

Rodgers' major concerns are: social and educational indicators of trends, developments and conditions in society, the elementary school as an institution, curricula and structures to attain set objectives, specific aspects of instructional programs in elementary settings, instructional support systems, and problems likely to confront the elementary school of the near future. Even experienced teachers, administrators, and supervisors of elementary schools are likely to find that this volume contains useful information on effective ways of contributing to the social and educational experience of students.

Saylor,** John Galen, and Joshua L. Smith, eds.

Removing Barriers to Humaneness in the High School. Washington, D.C.: Association for Supervision and Curriculum Development, NEA, 1971.

This collection of essays aims to improve the quality of education in the American secondary schools, by suggesting ways of overcoming some of the barriers to freedom and humanity.

Scott, Hugh Jerome. Messiah or Sacrificial Lamb: The Emerging Black School Superintendent. Washington, D.C.: Howard University Press, 1977.

The black school superintendent is a new personality in America's educational system. Scott focuses on seven black superintendents and the situation in which they find themselves, on the job and in the community. The book takes us to the heart of urban education, with its many challenges to policy-making and the problems accompanying the breakdown of urban centers.

Scott, John Irving Elias. Finding My Way. Boston: Meador Pub. Co., 1949.

This book is designed to prepare freshmen for college life. Scott discusses study skills, writing term papers, selecting the right vocation, preparing for and taking examinations, as well as other problems frequently encountered by college freshmen. Students will find much of the information still applicable in this day.

_____. Getting the Most Out of High School. Rev. ed. New York: Oceana Publications, Inc., 1967.

Scott speaks candidly about the meaning and advantages of a secondary school education and the unfortunate consequences of not grasping this opportunity. He traces the development of the high school, and its relation of other governmental agencies.

_____. *Living With Others: A Foundation Guidance Program for Junior HIgh and Upper Elementary Grades*. Boston: Meador Pub. Co., 1939.

Designed for use in upper elementary and junior high schools, this book reviews the aims of education, and presents teaching modules built around the seven cardinal principles of education.

_____. *Negro Students and Their Colleges*. Boston: Meador Publishing Co., 1949.

This book, consisting of three parts, is primarily addressed to black secondary students. In the first part the author cites various reasons for attending college. Part 2 consists of demographical data on various black colleges and includes a curriculum. The third part contains data on black enrollment and on graduates of non-black institutions.

Sedlacek,** William E., and Glenwood C. Brooks, Jr. *Racism in American Education: A Model for Change*. Chicago, Illinois: Nelson-Hall, 1976.

The authors show that most of the minority groups in America -- Afro-Americans, American Indians, Mexican Americans and Puerto Ricans -- have suffered from discrimination and racism in education. They suggest ways of eliminating this "institutional" racism. Presented in workshop format, the book contains a comprehensive bibliography and appendix of information on minorities in American society.

Shabazz, Abdul-Alin. *Fundamentals of Islamic Education*. Chicago: World Community of Islam in the West, 1977.

Based on articles published in *Muhammad Speaks* (now called *The Bilalian News*), this book deals with the development of a system of education for Islamic schools in the Muslim Community in America. He discusses general issues such as the purpose of education, as well as specific topics like education in prisons and adult education.

The introduction and epilogue by Farid Muhammad are excellent and contain the main thesis of the book, namely, that education must be ideologically oriented if it is to be useful in developing the World Community of Islam in the West.

Sherriffs, Alex C., and Kenneth Bancroft Clark. <u>How Relevant is Education in America Today</u>? Washington, D.C.: American Enterprise Institute for Public Policy Research, 1970.

This book consists of two lectures delivered during the Rational Debate Seminar in Washington, D.C. in 1970 and sponsored by the American Enterprise Institute. Also included are the rebuttals and finally the discussion session. A timely and enlightening discourse which merits the attention of educators, parents, and students alike.

Smith, Cynthia J., ed. <u>Advancing Equality of Opportunity: A Matter of Justice</u>. Washington, D.C.: Institute for the Study of Educational Policy, 1978.

Are affirmative action programs guilty of reverse discrimination? This and other questions dealing with the advancement of equality in America are addressed in these articles, originally presented at a conference held in Washington, D.C. in May 1977. In addition to the papers themselves, the follow-up discussions are also included. An introduction by Faustine Jones gives the reader a framework for the various papers presented. Among the participants are Kenneth Tollett, Charles Hamilton and other respected figures from government, academia, and the media.

Smith,* E. Brooks, Kenneth S. Goodman, and Robert Meredith.* <u>Language and Thinking in School</u>. 2nd ed. New York: Holt, Rinehart and Winston, 1976.

This book focuses on some modern views of language and linguistics, literature and symbolism, thinking and knowing. There are seven major parts, each of which concerns itself with an area of language and thinking. The first chapter of each section presents scholarly concepts drawn from related disciplines; and developes theoretical positions and practical applications for new and experienced teachers. Key recommendations to teachers are italicized.

Smith, Elsie J. <u>Counseling the Culturally Different Black Youth</u>. Columbus, Ohio: C. E. Merrill, 1973.

Smith emphasizes "action-orientated counseling techniques" over talk in dealing with black youths. She discusses the counselor's relationship to the families of the black students counseled. Smith explores a number of issues important to counseling black youths, including the role of educational counseling in vocational guidance and development. Smith also discusses some counseling theories and their relevance to the black student; the counselor in the 1970's and representative cases for discussion. The book also includes a bibliography.

Smitherman, Geneva. <u>Talkin' & Testifyin': The Language of Black America</u>. Boston: Houghton Mifflin, 1977.

Blacks and whites in the United States sometimes seem to speak different languages, and misunderstandings are bound to result. From African villages to Motown, from the sacred to the secular, the author draws on black culture in examining black speech. She illustrates her theories with the words of Frederick Douglas, Curtis Mayfield, W.E.B. DuBois, Claude Brown, Isaac Hayes, Richard Wright, and others. She offers as a remedy specific public policy suggestions that recognize the validity and make use of black English, such as a reading/language program that aims at fluency in both dialects.

Sommerville, Joseph C., and Linda L. BruckLacher.**
   <u>Selected Group Analysis of Administrative
   Field Experience Problems</u>. Toledo, Ohio:
   University of Toledo, 1973.

   This book describes the experiences of participants in the Administrative Field Experience Program at the University of Toledo. Problems commonly plaguing administrators and supervisors are analyzed. These include instructional leadership, philosophy and policy-making, school community relations, and routine administrative functions. The document is designed to serve as a resource and guide for administrative internship seminars.

   _____, and Robert Thiede.** <u>Contemporary
   Administrative and Supervisory Challenges:
   Analysis of Interesting Problems</u>. Toledo,
   Ohio: University of Toledo, 1976.

   This document grew out of the cooperative efforts of many individuals and evolves from numerous different school environments. Students, practitioners, and professors responded to each problem presented. Concepts, skills, and techniques which the student acquires in academic training are related to specific challenges which confront them in their field experiences. Several alternative approaches are considered for solving the problems. Although the publication does not offer definitive solutions to administrative problems, it does provide many tested approaches which are valuable to those who are faced with the challenges of School Administrations and Supervisions.

Sowell, Thomas. <u>Affirmative Action Reconsidered</u>.
   Was It Necessary in Academia? Washington, D.C.:
   American Enterprise Institute for Public Policy
   Research, 1975.

   This study accomplishes four major tasks: (1) It distinguishes between the basic concepts of affirmative action and many of the laws that arose out of the Affirmative Action label; (2) it measures the magnitude of the problem that Affirmative Action programs were meant to either solve or lessen; (3)

it considers the results of these programs; and
(4) it weighs the implications of Affirmative
Action policies for those directly involved as
well as for the general public. Vast literature
on such areas as education, employment, pay and
promotion are drawn upon in the study.

_____. Black Education: Myths and Tragedies.
New York: David McKay Co., Inc., 1972.

The author presents the experiences of the
Afro-American student on both black and white college campuses, and discusses the widespread academic policies such as the so-called "intelligence"
testing which tend to perpetuate myths and tragedies in the education of blacks. Sowell has proposals for solving some of these problems. His
personal experiences as a student and educator on
various college campuses (i.e. Cornell, Howard,
Harvard) makes for a powerful and provocative presentation of the total black educational experience
in America today.

Stent, Madelon Delany, and Frank Brown. Minorities
in U.S. Institutions of Higher Education. Washington: Praeger Press, 1977.

The book reviews minority college enrollment
and educational attainment in the United States.
Data on all major minority groups are listed separately by institutional type and control. Distinctions are also made between lower and upper division
enrollment, and among various fields and in major
professional schools. Socioeconomic characteristics
of the minority student population are also included.

_____, William R. Hazard,** and Harry N. Rivlin,** eds. Cultural Pluralism in Education:
A Mandate for Change. Dallas: Appleton-Century-Crofts, 1973.

This work compiled by Stent, Hazard, and Rivlin
contains a wealth of information on cultural pluralism in education and in the community. Essays are

contributed by respected scholars in the field of education. Rather than tending in the old direction of the melting pot theory, they propose a different kind of cultural pluralism in education, by suggesting we eliminate the present dichotomy between culture as taught in schools and the culture that exists in the community. Their recommendations are stimulating and insightful.

Strain, Lucille B. <u>Accountability in Reading Instruction</u>. Columbus, Ohio: Charles E. Merrill Publishing Co., 1976.

This book, addressed mainly to teachers of reading instruction, is in three major parts: (1) a description of the major aspects of accountability with applications to reading instructions; (2) a review of some basic procedures in reading instructions; and (3) a description of some reading skills and concepts. The text includes a glossary of the educational terms used throughout, as well as sample plans for reading instruction.

Sullivan,** Dorothy D., Beth Davey,** and Dolores Pawley Dickerson. <u>Games as Learning Tools, A Guide for Effective Use.</u> Paoli, Pennsylvania: Instructo/McGraw-Hill, 1978.

The book is a result of the authors' commitment to the concept that "classroom learning should and can be a positive experience for kids." Games, they argue, can contribute to this experience, and they proceed to show us just the kinds of games that can be designed and implemented in the classroom. The material comes from practical classroom and clinic usage, and can be adapted to suit individual classroom situations.

Tate, Elfleda Jackson. <u>Teaching the Disadvantaged</u>: <u>A Teacher's Manual.</u> Mountain View, Dakota: Peek Publications, 1971.

This book, a practical guide for teachers of disadvantaged children, describes disadvantaged learners, and recommends methods, materials, and content to help eradicate their deficits. Tate suggests ways to eliminate the trying situations which tend to defeat teachers of the disadvantaged.

    The emphasis is mainly on the lower-class Afro-American child. In the first part, Tate suggests ways of making elementary school curricula -- particularly reading, social studies, and health education -- more relevant to black children. In the second part, Tate examines the problems of discipline, classroom control, and the influence of black power on school children. Tate illustrates her suggestions with specific lesson plans.

Taylor, Ruth Sloan. <u>Teaching in the Desegregated Classroom</u>. West Nyack, New York: Parker Pub. Co., 1974.

    This study examines practical techniques, both tried and untried, for teaching in the desegregated classroom. It offers guidelines for assessing teacher values and developing positive activities for the students. Taylor suggests ways of improving student-to-student communication and incorporating minority group contributions into the curriculum. She gives methods of evaluating student progress, selecting the right materials and activities, and maintaining good after-classroom relationships between the students. Chapter 10 consists of twenty select questions and pertinent answers to the first nineteen of these questions on the subject of teaching in the desegregated classroom. The twentieth question is of particular interest, as only the reader can answer it.

Thompson, Daniel Calbert. <u>Private Black Colleges at the Crossroads</u>. Westport, Connecticut: Greenwood Press, 1974.

    This study presents some of the issues that arise in the survival of black colleges and universities, against a background of the rapidly changing American society and the rising expectations of black youth. Thompson asks whether black colleges are fulfilling their traditional goals, and takes a look at their students, faculty, curriculum, and their economic status. He then questions whether these institutions are worth saving.

Turner, Bridges Alfred. <u>From a Plow to a Doctorate - So What?</u> Hampton, Virginia: The Author, 1945.

    Using his own college experiences, Turner describes the difficulties encountered by blacks as they seek higher education. His main purpose, however, is to propose a plan for raising money for black scholarships. The plan is essentially to collect one dollar from at least one million people and then to invest funds to be used for scholarships for selected students. The end of the text includes a question sheet on the plan to be mailed back to the author for an assessment of his plan's feasibility.

Vontress, Clemmont E. <u>Counseling Negroes</u>. Boston: Houghton Mifflin Co., 1971.

    The author addresses himself to the special problems and concerns faced in the counseling of blacks in adolescence, preparation for college, adulthood and in the use of testing. The first section explores special tactics for counseling blacks. A very informative monograph.

Wallace, Walter L. <u>Student Culture: Social Structure and Continuity in a Liberal Arts College</u>. Chicago: Aldine Pub. Co., 1966.

    This study concerns itself with the phenomenon of assimilation or socialization, as it occurs on the campus of a small Midwestern liberal arts college. Socialization, Wallace argues, occurs at a faster rate than was believed by other social scientists. His conclusions center around a new social psychological technique. He uses a variation of the sociometric technique to characterize the interpersonal environments of each student of Midwest College. Included in Appendix 4 are questionnaires to study interests, attitudes of college students.

Walton, Sidney F., Jr. <u>The Black Curriculum: Developing a Program in Afro-American Studies</u>. East Palo Alto, California: Nairobi, 1969.

    Proposal for an academic paradigm exclusively designed for black individuals. The author discusses issues, past and present, confronting black students embodied in white America's educational system. At issue are various aspects of racism and an evaluation of the Afro-American Studies Program at Merritt College. The author also presents guidelines for developing relevant curriculum for blacks at all educational levels -- elementary, secondary and higher education. He also discusses the role of black educators.

Washington, Booker Taliaferro. <u>Working with the Hands: Being a Sequel to "Up From Slavery," Covering the Author's Experience in Industrial Training at Tuskegee</u>. New York: Doubleday, Page and Co., 1904.

    In this sequel to <u>Up From Slavery</u>, Washington puts forth his philosophy on the value of industrial training and the methods employed to develop it. He stresses that the objectives of education should be to upgrade the living conditions of its graduates or at least to make life more endurable for them. He strongly attacks the view that being educated means being free from hard work. While he stresses the need for industrial training, he maintains that this must be in conjunction with moral, religious, and mental education. The book is based on the vocational training for blacks as developed and instituted at Tuskegee Institute.

Watson, Bernard C. <u>In Spite of the System: the Individual and Educational Reform</u>. Cambridge, Mass.: Ballinger Pub. Co., 1974.

    The first half of this book is devoted to a discussion of the impact of education on society, public policy, and education, and an analysis of Christopher Jencks' <u>Inequality</u>. Watson also discusses the structural context of schools -- the principle's role, decentralization and community control.

Watson includes biographies of three individuals whose dynamic contributions in the field of education identify them as outstanding leaders.

Webster, Staten Wentford, ed. <u>The Disadvantaged Learner: Knowing, Understanding, Educating: A Collection of Original and Published Articles</u>. San Francisco: Chandler Pub. Co., 1966.

This book describes the disadvantaged learner, presents his educational problems, and provides a guideline to circumventing these problems. Designed as a reference for those concerned with urban education.

_____. <u>Discipline in the Classroom: Basic Principles and Problems</u>. San Francisco: Chandler Pub. Co., 1968.

Designed primarily for teachers, the book outlines in two parts the basic principles of classroom control while presenting in the latter part some very interesting test cases with both analyses and proposed solutions.

_____. <u>The Education of Black Americans</u>. New York: Intext Educational Publishers, 1974.

The book is divided into two parts, with the first giving a historical and contemporary outline of blacks in America and the second dealing mainly with the sociological aspects of blacks and education in the United States. The book primarily concerns the education of economically and socially disadvantaged blacks. It provides interesting data concerning the socio-economic and value systems of low-income blacks subjected to a white-oriented system.

Wesley, Charles H. <u>The History of Alpha Phi Alpha</u>:

A Development in Negro College Life. 2nd ed.
Washington, D.C.: Foundation Pub., 1939.

Alpha Phi Alpha is the oldest Afro-American college male fraternity. This book published in the thirties, considers the potential values of Afro-American college life especially in a select group as this. Based on documentation from primary sources, this history is a useful tool in the study of race history and Afro-American college life. Inside are graphic representations of some of the symbols of the fraternity along with pictures of outstanding members of the fraternity.

Whiting, Helen Adele. Primary Education. 2nd ed. Boston: The Christopher Publishing House, 1927.

A methods book containing model lesson plans and activities. The first part discusses general methods such as questioning and story telling, while the latter part of the book deals with more specific areas of methodology, such as math and music.

Wilcox, Preston. Integration or Separation in Education: K-12. New York: Afram Associates, 1969.

The primary subject dealt with in this research paper is the issue of educational integration, segregation and separation. Wilcox discusses the outcomes of integrated school systems, and the Black-Controlled School Movement. He provides evidence supporting the notion that educating for humanism is far more relevant than the issue of integrated or separatist education.

Wilkerson, Doxey A. Special Problems of Negro Education. Washington, D.C.: United States Government Printing Office, 1939.

The book is the result of research done in 1937 by the staff of the advisory committee to investigate public education in eighteen states which, at that time, required complete school segregation on all levels. Data used are primarily official publications and records for the years 1933 through 1936. The author focuses on the external aspects of public education such as the presence or absence of schools; their physical plant and resources; the attendance of children in school; the number, qualifications and salaries of teachers; pupil transportation; and financial support. Consideration is given to public elementary and secondary schools, to institutions of higher learning and to auxiliary educational programs (i.e. public library services, vocational education, rehabilitation services for the physically handicapped).

Williams, Eric Eustale. <u>Education in the British West Indies</u>. Port of Spain, Trinidad: Guardian Commerical Printery, 1950.

This book calls for the creation of a university for West Indian students throughout the Caribbean. It is directed at educators and administrators in the hope that they would see the need for such an institution. Various forms of education at different levels are analyzed with a view to expanding the existing system to include a university system. An official report on higher education in British colonies is included to reinforce arguments for the establishment of a university that would meet the needs of all students.

Williams, Lucius L. and Jerome Kaplan,** <u>Student's Self-Directing Computational Guide I</u>. New York: Random House, 1974.

This computational guidebook consists of mathematical exercises to be used as a review of basic skills. Because of the model examples, "Quick Check" sections, and the answer sections, the guidebook can be used with the aid of a teacher or independently. Guide I contains practice exercises on whole numbers, fractions and decimals which include practice in adding, subtracting, multiplying and dividing.

_____. *Student's Self-Directing Computational Guide II*. New York: Random House, 1974.

Like Guide I, Guide II consists of mathematical exercises to be used as a review of basic skills, and can be used with the aid of a teacher or independently. Guide II contains practice exercises on whole numbers, integers, rational numbers (fractions and decimals in both positive and negative form), equations, proportions, and percentages. Again practice in adding, subtracting, multiplying and dividing is included.

Williams, William Taylor Burwell. *Duplication of Schools for Negro Youth*. Lynchburg, Virginia: J. P. Bell Company Inc., 1914.

The author emphasizes the need for greater efficiency in the school systems in the South. There should be the dire effort of preventing the unwise use of means and efforts of other people and a reduction of "rivalries, divisions, jealousies, and other evils" resulting from unnecessary duplication of Southern schools for blacks. He lists fifty instances of misappropriations of funds and efforts in the duplication of these schools. The book includes charts and tables of these fifty duplicated schools.

_____. *Report on Negro Universities in the South*. New Orleans: Tulane University Press, 1913.

This pre-World War I study of black universities in the South was undertaken to determine the nature of the work of the black universities at that time. The data were collected from twenty-two reputable black colleges with campuses scattered over ten Southern states and the District of Columbia. The work done by these universities covers every phase of education from the lowest elementary school grade up to college work. Areas investigated were length of terms, college entrance requirements, courses of study, administration, instruction, and relative costs of college departments. The author also lists the six best black

Universities in the South as Howard, Fisk, Virginia Union, Atlanta, Shaw, and Wiley. There are tables in the book drawn to represent the different areas studied.

Willie, Charles Vert. <u>Race Mixing in the Public Schools</u>. New York: Praeger, 1973.

Willie examines the bases for success and failure in integrated education. He explores integration situations in two elementary schools and two junior high schools. The purpose of the study is to discover patterns of social adjustment in young children.

_____. <u>The Sociology of Urban Education</u>. Lexington, Mass.: Lexington Books, 1978.

The author holds the view that because the United States is essentially urban, its educational system must be essentially urban as well. He then shows how pluralism is the essence of an urban society. The educational system can meet the needs of contemporary America only by educating students for life in a pluralistic community and developing in them a sense of community among heterogeneous and diversified people. This is to be achieved through a conceptual approach to desegregation and integration, rather than the trial and error technique which has prevailed.

The book is divided into four parts. Part one discusses urban education issues, part two, education planning and policymaking, part three, desegregating elementary and secondary schools and part four, integrating colleges and universities.

_____, and Ronald R. Edmonds, eds. <u>Black Colleges in America</u>. New York: Teachers College Press, 1978.

This book contains papers presented at the Black College Conference held at Harvard Graduate School of Education in March and April 1976. The sixteen papers are presented in three parts. Part

one deals with history and purpose of black
colleges; part two deals with the administration,
financing, and governance of black colleges; and
part three deals with teaching and learning. Each
part is preceeded by an overview which sets a
frame of reference for the papers presented in
that section. The authors describe this work as
"a serious effort to lay before the public an analysis of what black colleges and universities do
for themselves and for the nation." The papers
are varied and reflect the diversified backgrounds
of their contributors, who include such notables
as Benjamin E. Mays, Samuel DuBois Cook, and Daniel
C. Thompson.

_____, and Arline Sakuma McCord.* Black
   Students at White Colleges. New York:
   Praeger, 1972.

Originally a study of white colleges in upper
New York, the authors examine, from the students'
point of view, the still little-explored area of
black students on predominantly white college campuses. The reader will find the authors' methodology and conclusions of special interest.

Wilson, Charles H., Sr. Education for Negroes in
   Mississippi Since 1910: An Historical Approach.
   Boston: Meador Publishing Co., 1947.

A well-documented treatise of the elementary,
secondary, and post-secondary educational institutions in Mississippi for the Afro-American from
1910 to 1947. The author includes chapters on
Afro-American teachers, the general high school
curriculum, the financing of such schools, as well
as industrial, vocational, religious, athletic,
and music education in the state.

The volume provides an excellent reference
source for those in the field of education and Afro-
American history.

Wilson, Thomasyne Lightfoote. Toward Viable Directions in Postsecondary Education: Nontraditional/Unconventional Education Through a "Community-Family" Context. San Francisco, California: Sapphire Publishing Co., 1976.

This book puts forward some viable directions for secondary education. The author finds that prospects for equality in postsecondary education are good. She argues, however, that postsecondary education should include the whole community, and that the values, goals, processes and assessments of and for education should come from the "realities" of non-traditional students and not simply from the "privileged". The book contains several schema, diagrams, tables, and also an appendix containing an evaluative instrumentation for educational programs.

Woodard, Samuel L., ed. Reducing Stress on Black Administrators. New York: Vantage Press, Inc., 1978.

Papers presented at a conference on "Creative Leadership" sponsored by Howard University form the bulk of this book. Part one, by James P. Comer, and part two, by Maurice C. Woodard and Charles W. Harris, contain very good analyses of the pressure-building situations faced by most administrators and black administrators in particular. The third and last part consists of exercises for administrators to reduce stress using the Transactional Analysis Approach. A short book (forty pages) but full of useful information.

Woodson, Carter Goodwin. The Education of the Negro Prior to 1861: A History of the Education of the Colored People of the United States from the Beginning of Slavery to the Civil War. New York: G. P. Putnam's Sons, 1915.

Focusing on the education of the Afro-American in the antebellum period, the author starts from the inception of slavery where education was denied the Afro-American. The history of the antebellum covers two periods. The first period extends from the time of the introduction of slavery to the climax of the insurrectionary movement about 1835. The second period extends from the time when the industrial revolution changed slavery from a patriarchal to an economic institution and when intelligent blacks, encouraged by abolitionists, made so many attempts to organize servile insurrections that the pendulum began to swing the other way.

The early advocates of the education of blacks were of three classes: first, masters who desired to increase the economic efficiency of their labor supply; second, sympathetic persons who wished to help the oppressed; and, third, zealous missionaries who taught the slave the English language that they might learn the principles of the Christian Religion.

_____. The Mis-Education of the Negro. Washington, D.C.: First published 1933, Associated Publisher, Inc. Reissued, 1969 and 1972, Associated Publishers Inc.

Woodson, who was the founder of the famous Journal of Negro History, describes the blighting effects which the American educational system has had on blacks. Woodson argued that the aim of education was to transform the Negro, not to develop him as through the study of his own culture and history. With books like this one, published in 1933, Woodson did much to encourage the teaching of black history in the schools.

Woolfolk, E. Oscar, and Sherman Jones.* Planning the Academic Program. Washington, D.C.: Institute for Services to Education, 1973.

The monograph presents the results of the work by the office of Cooperative Academic Planning with a number of traditional black colleges, over a period of two years. The first part is a conceptual framework for academic planning; the second part concerns curricular analysis. The bibliography offers a wealth of references for those in education interested in the areas of curriculum development and academic planning.

>_____, eds. Curriculum Change in Black Colleges: A Report on the Cooperative Academic Planning Curriculum Development Conference. Washington, D.C.: Institute for Services to Education, 1972.

This book is the result of the "Curriculum Change in Black Colleges" conference held in 1972. It includes the presentations of the various speakers and selected excerpts from the discussions. The speakers represent faculty and staff from some twenty-five black colleges and include such people as Elias Blake, Harold Delaney, and Edward Brantley. Topics discussed include new directions in black colleges, deparochializing general education, nontraditional study, and implementing curriculum change.

>_____, eds. Focus on Curriculum Change in Black Colleges II: A Report on the Cooperative Academic Planning Curriculum Development Workshop. Washington, D.C.: Institute for Services to Education, 1972.

This book is a report on the second workshop held by the Cooperative Academic Planning Program and consists of papers presented in the five plenary sessions (part I), synopses of four educational systems which address themselves to the educational needs of students at black colleges (part II), and summaries of curriculum documents prepared by each team.

The contributing speakers are indigenous experts from various black colleges as well as from the broader higher education community and include such notables as George Owens, Albert Berrian, Renee Westcott, and Joseph Katz. Topics discussed include the black college as a manpower resources delivery system, an academic skills center, and the developmental perspective in higher education.

_____, and Joel O. Nwagbaraocha,* eds.
Curriculum Change in Black Colleges III: A
Report on Two Cooperative Academic Planning
Curriculum Development Workshops. Washington,
D.C.: Institute for Services to Education,
1973.

The papers contained in this book are the
result of two workshops held in Atlanta, Georgia
by the office of Cooperative Academic Planning in
cooperation with its consortial colleges. These
workshops were held in 1972 and 1973, and reflect
an attempt by black colleges to effect programs
which deal with current problems in America today.
Contributors in this volume include Margaret
Alexander, James Parker, Eddie Martin, and Lillie
Davis. Topics discussed include humanities with
a black focus, development of urban-related programs in black colleges, and accelerated curricular change on black campuses.

_____, and Roosevelt Calbert.* Curriculum
Change in Black Colleges IV: A Report on
Two Cooperative Academic Planning Curriculum Development Workshops. Washington, D.C.:
Institute for Services to Education, 1973.

Consist of proceedings of two workshops:
December 4-6, 1972 orientation workshop for over
fifty consortial schools, and the June 4-13, 1973
summer workshop in Dallas, Texas for the same colleges and universities. Topics include: (1) "Past
Goals, Present Mission and Future Prospects for
Our Colleges and Universities"; (2) "Freshman Interdisciplinary Program at Fisk University"; (3) "Performance-Based Instructional Programs: A Realistic
Approach Toward Developing and Implementing";
(4) "The Black Colleges in Transition"; (5) "Academic Skills Center." In addition, abstracts of
curriculum documents are also included.

Elias Blake, Jr., Hugh Gloster, and Broadus N.
Butler are among the contributors.

Wright, Nathan, Jr., ed. What Black Educators Are

Saying. New York: Hawthorn Books, Inc., 1970.

A collection of essays contributed by prominent black educators, such as C. Eric Campbell and Preston Wilcox. The anthology is divided into 5 parts: I. The black educator, II. The white Establishment, III. The University Scene, IV. The Educational Redefinition, and V. Community Involvement and Action.

A section containing brief introductions of the contributors is also contained in the volume. Collectively these educators present substantial insight into the critical issues faced by blacks in all aspects of education.

Wright, Richard Robert. A Brief Historical Sketch of Negro Education in Georgia. Savannah, Georgia: Robinson Printing House, 1894.

A brief but informative record of Afro-American education in Georgia spaning the times of clandestine "school" meetings to the founding of such prominent universities as Morris Brown, Spelman, and Clark. The monograph tells of the influences of the various denominations and missionaries in establishing a formidable educational system. A review of the public schools in major cities, the quality of education, and the students contribute to this excellent chronicle of the history of education for the Afro-American in Georgia.

Young,** Beverly Sue, Mary Hilton Appleberry,** and Odis Odean Rhodes. Reading How and Why. Dubuque, Iowa: Kendall/Hunt, 1976.

Reading How and Why, a handbook on reading, offers the typical classroom teacher concrete and practical suggestions on teaching techniques and materials in specific areas of reading instruction.

Young,** Ethel, and Natelkka Burrell. Forward March. Mountain View, California: Pacific Press Publishing Association, 1963.

This book is designed for the fifth grade reading level and includes many interesting short stories as well as a useful glossary. A booklet of tests is also available for this book. This book was developed by the Department of Education General Conference of Seventh-day Adventists.
In the same series there are other readers for the different levels.

Notes

¹The Library of Congress classification system was used in determining which books should be included in this field.

²Newby, James Edward. "Equality of Educational Opportunity: Content Analysis of Six Selected Negro Authors, 1960-1970." Unpublished Doctoral Dissertation, University of Southern California, 1974; Wright, Nathan, Jr., ed. What Black Educators Are Saying. New York: Hawthorn Books, Inc., 1970.

³Examples include: McPherson,* James M., Laurence B. Holland,* James M. Banner, Jr.,* Nancy J. Weiss,* Michael D. Bell.* Blacks in America: Bibliographical Essays. Garden City, New York: Doubleday & Co., Inc., 1971; Miller, Elizabeth W.,* compiler. The Negro in America: A Bibliography. Cambridge, Mass.: Harvard University Press, 1966; Porter, Dorothy Burnett. Early American Negro Writings: A Bibliographical Study. Bibliographical Society of America Papers, Vol. 39, Third Quarter, 1945; West,** Earle H., compiler. A Bibliography of Doctoral Research on the Negro, 1933-1966. Ann Arbor, Michigan: Xerox, University Microfilms, 1969.

⁴Verification of an author's ethnic identity included: appearance of author's photograph in publication(s); my personal knowledge of the author; indication of ethnicity in the card catalog of the Moorland-Spingarn Research Center, Howard University; identified in biographical directories on blacks such as Shockley and Chandler's Living Black American Authors: A Biographical Directory; Robinson, International Library of Negro Life and History: Historical Negro Biographies; Matney, Who's Who Among Black Americans; Rush, Black American Writers Past and Present; or two or more indications of ethnicity through personal knowledge of individuals who recommended authors to be included in the bibliography. One asterisk (*) indicates coauthor's ethnic identity was not verified. Two asterisks (**) indicate coauthor is non-black.

Selected Bibliography

Davis, Arthur Paul. *From the Dark Tower: Afro-American Writers from 1900 to 1960.* Washington, D.C.: Howard University Press, 1974.

Fischer,* Russell G. "James Baldwin: A Bibliography, 1947-1962." *Bulletin of Bibliography* 24 (January-April, 1965), 127-130.

Matney, William C., ed. *Who's Who Among Black Americans.* 1st ed. 1975-1976 Vol. 1. Northbrook, Illinois: Who's Who Among Black Americans, Inc. Publishing Co., 1976.

Porter, Dorothy Burnett, compiler. *A Working Bibliography on the Negro in the United States.* Ann Arbor, Michigan: Xerox, University Microfilms, 1969.

Robinson, Wilhelmena S. *International Library of Negro Life and History: Historical Negro Biographies.* New York: Publishers Co., Inc., 1967.

Rush, Theressa Gunnels, et. al. *Black American Writers Past and Present.* Metuchen, New Jersey: Scarecrow Press, Inc., 1975.

Shockley, Ann Allen and Sue P. Chandler. *Living Black American Authors: A Biographical Directory.* New York: R. R. Bowker Co., 1973.

Trent, Toni. "Stratification Among Blacks by Black Authors." *Negro History Bulletin* 34 (December, 1971), 179-181.

AUTHOR INDEX

Abramowitz, Elizabeth A., 1
Anderson,** Archibald W., 17
Anthony, Earl, 1
Appleberry,** Mary Hilton, 80
Arnez, Nancy Levi, 1-2
Bacote, Clarence A., 2
Bailey,** Judity, 19
Baker, Gwendolyn C., 20
Ballard, Allen B., 2
Banks, James A., 2-4
Bibens,** Robert F., 39
Blackwell, James Edward, 4-5
Bloom,** Benjamin S., 5
Bond, Horace Mann, 5-6
Bonner, Mary Winstead, 6-7
Bowles,** Frank, 7
Boyd, William M., 7
Brawley, Benjamin Griffith, 8
Brawley, James Philip, 8-9
Brazziel, William F., 9
Britts, Maurice W., 10
Brooks, Charlotte Kendrick, 10
Brooks, Glenwood C., Jr., 61
Brown, Charles Allen, 10
Brown, Frank, 65
Brown, Hugh Victor, 10-11
Browne, Rose Butler, 11
Brucklacher,** Linda L., 64
Bryant, Spurgeon Quinton, 11-12
Bullock, Henry Allen, 12
Burrell, Leon F., 12-13, 17
Burrell, Natelkka, 80-81
Calbert,* Roosevelt, 79
Caldwell, Dista H., 15
Caliver, Ambrose, 13-14
Campbell, Thomas Monroe, 15
Cary, Willie Mae, 15-16
Castañeda,* Alfredo, 16
Cheek, James E., 16
Clark, Felton Grandison, 16-17
Clark, Kenneth Bancroft, 17, 62
Clements,** Zacharie J., 17
Clift, Virgil A., 17
Clifton, Fred J., 17-18

Cogdell, Roy Thomas, 18
Coger, Rick, 18
Colson, Edna Meade, 19
Conley, Houston, 19
Cozart, Leland Stanford, 19-20
Crawford, George Williamson, 20
Cross, Dolores E., 20
Culp, Daniel Wallace, 20-21
Dabney, Lillian Gertrude, 21
Daniel, Walter Green, 21
Dansby, B. Baldwin, 21-22
Davey,** Beth, 66
Davidson, Edmonia White, 22
Davis, Allison, 5, 22-23
DeCosta, Frank, 7
Delaney, William H., 23
Della-Dora,** Delmo, 23
Derbigny, Irving Antony, 23-24
Dickerson, Dolores Pawley, 66
Dill,* Augustus Granvill, 24
DuBois, William Edward Burghardt, 24
Edmonds, Ronald R., 74-75
Edwards, Harry, 24
Edwards, Norma S., 25
Edwards, Thomas Bentley, 25-26
English,* James W., 11
Epps, Edgar G., 26-27, 34
Eugene, Georgia, 19
Favors, Aaron, 29-30
Fisher,* Margaret Barrow, 27-28
Flemming, John E., 28
Foster, Marcus A., 28-29
Froe, Otis D., 29
Froe,* Otyce B., 29
Gary, Lawrence E., 29-30
Gayles, Anne Richardson, 30
Giles, Raymond H., Jr., 30-31
Gill, Gerald R., 28
Glasgow, Ann Duncan, 31
Goodman, Kenneth S., 62-63
Goodwin, Bennie Eugene, 31
Gordon, Edmund Wyatt, 32, 52
Grambs,** Jean D., 3-4
Green, Robert Lee, 32-34
Greene, Harry Washington, 34
Gurin,** Patricia, 34
Hankins, Lela Ruth, 35
Harper, Fredrick Douglass, 35

Harris, Marquis Lafayette, 35
Harris,* Norene, 35-36
Haskins, James, 36
Haynes, Carrie Ayers, 36
Haynes, Leonard L., III, 37
Hazard,** William R., 65-66
Heilman,** Arthur W., 37-38
Henderson, George, 38-39, 58
Hendrick,** Irving G., 39
Hesburgh,** Theodore Martin, 39-40
Hess,** Robert E., 5
Holley, Joseph Winthrop, 40
Holmes, Dwight Oliver Wendell, 40
Holmes, Elizabeth Ann, 37-38
House, James E., 23
Hudson, Herman C., 40
Hullfish,** Gordon H., 17
Hunter, William Andrew, 40-41
Hurst, Charles G., Jr., 41
Jackson, John Henry, 41
Jackson, Nathaniel, 35-36
James, Richard L., 16
Johnson, Charles Spurgeon, 41-42
Johnson, Harry Alleyn, 42
Johnson, Kenneth R., 42
Johnson, Roosevelt, 42-43
Johnson, Simon Otis, 43-44
Johnson, Sylvia T., 44
Jones, Edward Allen, 44-45
Jones, Gilbert Haven, 45
Jones, Leon, 45
Jones, Reginald Lanier, 39, 46
Jones,* Sherman, 77-79
Joyce,* William W., 4
Kaplan,** Jerome, 72
Key,** June, 19
Kimmons, Willie James, 46-47
Knox, Ellis O., 47
Lee,** Maurice A., 29
LeMelle, Tilden J., 47
LeMelle, Wilbert J., 47
Levine,** Daniel U., 56
Lewis, James, Jr., 47-48
Lightfoot, Sara L., 48
Logan, Rayford Whittingham, 49
MacMillan,** Donald L., 46
Maupin, Madeline Taylor, 49
Mays, Benjamin Elijah, 49

Mays, Robert E., 50
McAllister, Jane Ellen, 50
McCord, Arline Sakuma, 75
McKinney, Richard Ishmael, 50-51
McKinney, Theophilus Elisha, 51
Mercer, Walter Alexander, 51-52
Meredith,* Robert, 62-63
Miller, LaMar P., 52
Miller,* Paul A., 39-40
Minnis, Bernard, 19
Moore, William, Jr., 52-54
Moseley, Clifton L., 54
Muhammad, Farid I., 54
Napper, George, 54-55
Newton, James E., 55
Neyland, Leedell Wallace, 55
Noble, Jeanne L., 27, 55-56
Nwagbaraocha,* Joel O., 79
Ornstein,* Allan C., 56
Payne, Charles Ray, 56-57
Perry, Thelma Davis, 57
Phillips, Carol, 57
Picott, John Rupert, 57-58
Plotkin,** Lawrence, 17
Pruitt, Anne S., 58
Rackley, Larney, G., 30
Ragan,* William Burke, 58
Redbury,** Dennis, 56-57
Rembert, Emma White, 58-59
Rhodes, Odis Odean, 80
Richmond, Mossie J., Jr., 59
Riley,* John W., 55
Rivlin,** Harry N., 65-66
Robbins,* Webster, 16
Rodgers, Frederick A., 59
Rydingsword,* Carl E., 35-36
Saylor,** John Galen, 59-60
Scott, Hugh Jerome, 60
Scott, John Irving Elias, 60-61
Sedlacek,** William E., 61
Shabazz, Abdul-Alim, 61-62
Sherriffs,* Alex C., 62
Sitaram,** K., 18
Smith, Cynthia J., 62
Smith,* E. Brooks, 62-63
Smith, Elsie J., 63
Smith, Joshua L., 59-60

Smitherman, Geneva, 63
Sommerville, Joseph C., 64
Sowell, Thomas, 64-65
Stent, Madelon Delany, 65-66
Stiles,** Lindley J., 20
Strain, Lucille B., 66
Sullivan,** Dorothy D., 66
Swinton, David H., 28
Tate, Elfleda Jackson, 66-67
Taylor, Ruth Sloan, 67
Thiede,** Robert T., 64
Thompson, Daniel Calbert, 67-68
Turner, Bridges Alfred, 68
Vontress, Clemmont E., 68
Wagstaff, Lonnie H., 53-54
Wallace, Walter L., 68
Walton, Sidney F., Jr., 69
Washington, Booker Taliaferro, 69
Watson, Bernard C., 69-70
Webster, Staten Wentford, 70
Wesley, Charles H., 70-71
Wharton, Clifton R., 39-40
Whiting, Helen Adele, 71
Wilcox, Preston, 71
Wilkerson, Doxey A., 32, 56, 71-72
Williams, Eric Eustale, 72
Williams, Lucius L., 72
Williams, William Taylor Burwell, 73-74
Willie, Charles Vert, 74-75
Wilson,* Alan B., 26
Wilson, Charles H., Sr. 75
Wilson, Thomasyne Lightfoote, 75-76
Wirt,* Frederick, 26
Woodard, Samuel L., 76
Woodson, Carter Godwin, 76-77
Woolfolk, E. Oscar, 77-79
Wright, Nathan, Jr., 79-80
Wright, Richard Robert, 80
Young,** Beverly Sue, 80
Young,** Ethel, 80-81

TITLE INDEX

Access of Black Students to Graduate and Professional Schools, 4

Accountability in Reading Instruction, 66

Administering the Individualized Instruction Program, 47-48

Advancing Equality of Opportunity, 62

Affirmative Action Reconsidered, 64-65

Against the Odds, 52-53

Alternative Strategies, 58-59

America's Other Children, 38

An Analysis of the Arkansas-Georgia Statewide Desegregation Plans, 37

An Analysis of the Specific References to Negroes in Selected Curricula for the Education of Teachers, 19

Appraising Teacher Performance, 48

Attitudes of High School Students as Related to Success in School, 25

A Background Study of Negro College Students, 13

Between Two Worlds, 7

Biology: A Problem Solving Approach, 35

Black Administrators in Public Community Colleges, 46-47

Black Agenda for Career Education, 42-43

Black American Scholars--A Study of Their Beginnings, 5

The Black College, 47

Black Colleges in America, 74-75

Black Consciousness, Identity, and Achievement, 34

The Black Curriculum, 69

Black Education: Myths and Tragedies, 65

Black Educators in White Colleges, 53-54

Black Leadership in Urban Schools, 31

Black Manifesto for Education, 36

Black Scholars on Higher Education in the 70's, 43

Black Self-Concept, 3-4

Black Students, 24

Black Students at White Colleges, 75

Black Students in White Schools, 26-27

Black Students: White Campus, 35

Black Studies in Public Schools, 30-31

Blacker Than Thou, 54-55

Blacks on White College Campuses, 10

Blind Man on a Freeway, 53

Born to Rebel, 49

A Brief Historical Sketch of Negro Education in Georgia, 80

A Brief History of Jackson College, 21-22

A Candle in the Dark: A History of Morehouse, 44-45

The Case for Affirmative Action for Blacks in Higher Education, 28

The Clark College Legacy, 8-9

Collective Monologues I, 57

College Education as Personal Development, 27-28

The Common School and the Negro American, 24

Community College Response to the High-Risk Student, 53

Compensatory Education for the Disadvantaged, 32

Compensatory Education for Cultural Deprivation, 5

Contemporary Administrative and Supervisory Challenges, 64

Contingency Planning for a Unitary School System, 19

The Control of State-Supported Teacher-Training Programs for Negroes, 16-17

Counseling Negroes, 68

Counseling the Culturally Different Black Youth, 63

A Critical Examination of the Adams Case, 37

Cultural Pluralism, 27

Cultural Pluralism in Education, 65-66

Curriculum Change in Black Colleges, 78

Curriculum Change in Black Colleges III, 79

Curriculum Change in Black Colleges IV, 79

A Curriculum Evaluation of Black Studies in Relation to Student Knowledge of Afro-American History and Culture, 55

Curriculum and Instruction in the Elementary School, 59

Darl, 17-18

Democracy and the District of Columbia Public Schools, 47

Desegregating America's College, 7

Developing Effective Instructional Systems, 18

Diary of a Harlem School Teacher, 36

The Disadvantaged Learner, 70

Discipline in the Classroom, 70

Dr. Dillard of the Jeanes Fund, 8

Duplication of Schools for Negro Youth, 73

The Easy Way to Better Grades, 29

Education and the Cultural Crisis, 41

Education and the Segregation Issue, 40

Education for an Open Society, 23

Education for Negroes in Mississippi Since 1910, 75

Education for Peace, 38-39

Education in the British West Indies, 72

Education in Theory and Practice, 45

The Education of Black Americans, 70

The Education of Black Folk, 2

Education of Negro Teachers, 13

The Education of the Negro Child, 15

Education of the Negro in the American Social Order, 5-6

The Education of the Negro Prior to 1861, 76-77

The Educational Needs of Minority Groups, 16

The Educational Status of Children During the First School Year Following Four Years of Little or no Schooling, 32-33

The Educational Status of Children in a District Without Public Schools, 33

Educators Diagnostic Guidebook, 6-7

The Emergence of Black Colleges, 31

E-Qual-ity Education in North Carolina Among Negroes, 10-11

Equality of Educational Opportunity, 52

The Evolution of the Negro College, 40

Family and Personal Development in Adult Basic Education, 22

Finding My Way, 60

Focus on Curriculum Change in Black Colleges II, 78

Forward March, 80-81

Foundations of American Education, 58

Foundations of Intercultural Communication, 18

From a Plow to a Doctorate - So What?, 68

From Brown to Boston, 45

Fundamentals of Islamic Education, 61-62

Games as Learning Tools, A Guide for Effective Use, 66

General Education in the Negro College, 23-24

Getting the Most Out of High School, 60

Good Morning Mrs. "B", 43

Good News on Grape Street, 36

Higher Education Among Negroes, 51

Higher Education's Responsibility for Advancing Equality, 16

The History of Alpha Phi Alpha, 70-71

History of Education from the Greeks to the Present Time, 41

The History of Florida Agricultural and Mechanical University, 55

A History of Negro Education in the South: From 1619 To the Present, 12

History of Morehouse College, 8

The History of Schools for Negroes in the District of Columbia, 1807-1947, 21

History of the American Teachers Association, 57

A History of the Education of Negroes in North Carolina, 11

History of the Virginia Teachers Association, 57

Holders of Doctorates Among American Negroes, 34

Howard University: The First Hundred Years 1867-1967, 49

How Relevant is Education in America Today, 62

How to Become a Successful Student, 29

How to Make it in College, 40

Humanizing the Desegregated School, 51

In Spite of the System, 69-70

Instructional Planning in the Secondary School, 30

The Integration of American Schools, 35-36

Integration or Separation in Education, 71

Introduction to American Education, 38

Islamic Social and Educational Issues, 54

Issues in Year-Round Education, 59

Language and Thinking in School, 62-63

Learn By Doing, 23

The Lengthening Shadow of Slavery, 28

Living with Others, 61

Love My Children, 11

Making Schools Work, 28-29

The "Measurement Mystique", 44

Messiah or Sacrificial Lamb, 60

Minorities in U.S. Institutions of Higher Education, 65

The Mis-Education of the Negro, 77

The Movable School Goes to the Negro Farmer, 15

Multi-Cul, 56

Multi-Cultural Education Clinic Papers, 56-57

Multicultural Education Through Competency-Based Teacher Education, 40-41

Multicultural Elementary Classrooms, 43-44

Multimedia Materials for Afro-American Studies, 42

National Survey of the Higher Education of Negroes, 13

The Negro College Graduate, 42

Negro Education in Alabama, 6

Negro Education in America, 17

The Negro Student at Integrated Colleges, 17

Negro Students and Their Colleges, 61

The Negro Woman's College Education, 55-56

New Directions in Special Education, 46

New Students and Coordinated Counseling, 58

Opening the Public School Curriculum, 50

Operation Cope, 22

The Origin and Development of Secondary Education for Negroes, 10

The Participation of Blacks in Graduate and Professional Schools, 4-5

Partners in Urban Education, 1-2

Passport to Freedom, 41

Patterns for Lifelong Learning, 39-40

Peer Group Counseling Policies and Human-Relations Workshops Procedures, 49

A Personnel Study of Negro College Students, 13-14

Planning the Academic Program, 77

Primary Education, 71

Private Black Colleges at the Crossroads, 67-68

Problems and Issues in Education of Exceptional Children, 46

Proceedings from the National Invitational Conference on Racial & Ethnic Data, 1

Profiles, 17

Proven and Promising Educational Innovations in Secondary Schools, 30

Quality Education for All Americans, 9

A Quarter Century of Black Experience in Elementary and Secondary Education, 1950-1975, 57-58

Race Mixing in the Public Schools, 74

Racial Crisis in American Education, 32

Racism in American Education, 61

Reading How and Why, 80

The Reading Interests and Needs of Negro College Freshmen Regarding Social Science Materials, 21

Really Reading, 37

Reducing Stress on Black Administrators, 76

Reforming Metropolitan Schools, 56

The Regional Project in Secondary Education, 25-26

Religion in Higher Education Among Negroes, 50-51

Removing Barriers to Humaneness in the High School, 59-60

Report on Negro Universities in the South, 73-74

Restructuring the Educational Process, 29-30

School Desegregation in the North, 26

School Desegregation - Making it Work, 33-34

The Search for Talent, 6

Secondary Education for Negroes, 14

Selected Group Analysis of Administrative Field Experience Problems, 64

Smuggling Language into the Teaching of Reading, 37-38

Social Class Influences upon Learning, 22-23

The Sociology of Urban Education, 74

A Special Delivery, 25

Special Education in Transition, 46

Special Problems of Negro Education, 71-72

The Story of Atlanta University, 2

Student Culture, 68

Student Dissent in the Schools, 39

Student's Self-Directing Computational Guide I, 72

Student's Self-Directing Computational Guide II, 73

A Study of Some Social and Psychological Factors Influencing Educational Achievement, 26

Supervising Student Teachers, 50

A Survival Kit for Brothers & Sisters Going to Grey Colleges, 12-13

Talkin' & Testifyin', 63

The Talladega Manual of Vocational Guidance, 20

Teachers Should Care, 39

Teaching in a Multi-Cultural Society, 20

Teaching in the Desegregated Classroom, 67

Teaching in the Desegregated School, 51-52

Teaching Social Studies to Culturally Different Children, 4

Teaching Strategies for Ethnic Studies, 2-3

Teaching Strategies for the Social Studies, 3

Teaching the Black Experience, 3

Teaching the Culturally Disadvantaged, 42

Teaching the Disadvantaged, 66-67

The Testing of Black Students, 51

The Time of the Furnaces, 1

The Torch Glows, 54

They Can Learn English, 10

Toward Viable Directions in Postsecondary Education, 75-76

The Tragedies in American Education, 48

Training of Negro Teachers in Louisiana, 50

Twentieth Century Negro Literature, 20-21

Two Centuries of Methodist Concern, 9

The Urban Challenge, 32

A Venture of Faith, 19-20

Vocational Education and Guidance of Negroes, 14

The Voice in the Wilderness, 35

The West Indian Experience in British Schools, 31

What Black Educators Are Saying, 79-80

Working with the Hands, 69

Worlds Apart, 48

Worse Than Silence: The Black Child's Dilemma, 15-16

Why I Don't Like Bussing, 11-12

ABOUT THE AUTHOR

James Edward Newby is assistant Professor of Foundations of Education at Howard University, Washington, D.C. He has taught at Los Angeles Harbor College, El Camino College, Pepperdine University, and California State University at Long Beach. Born in Oakland, Tennessee, he grew up and received his public-school education in Memphis, Tennessee. After completing military service in the United States Army, he obtained his A.A. degree at Los Angeles City College, his B.A. degree at California State University Los Angeles, his M.A. at California State University Long Beach, and his Ed.D. degree from the University of Southern California.

Dr. Newby holds membership in such professional organizations as the American Educational Research Association, American Educational Studies Association, American Sociological Association, National Alliance of Black School Educators, and Phi Delta Kappa. His list of publications include, "Black Authors in Philosophy, Psychology, and Religion: An Annotated Bibliography of Books"; and "Black Authors: An Annotated Bibliography of Autobiographies and Biographies." Dr. Newby is a recipient of several awards for community service and is listed in Community Leaders and Noteworthy Americans (1976-1977).